ENGLISH COUNTRY HOUSE STYLE

TRADITIONS, SECRETS, AND UNWRITTEN RULES

Milo & Katy Campbell

Photography by Mark Nicholson

ABRAMS, NEW YORK

Contents

Introduction

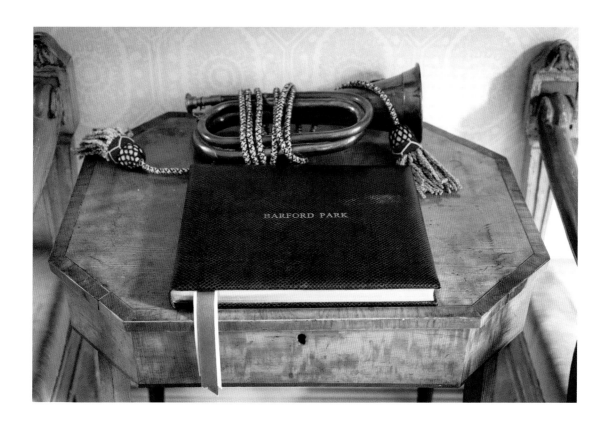

There are certain motifs unique to English country houses. These may be specific rooms, architectural details, decorative flourishes, or arrangements of furniture, but all are unmistakably synonymous with that peculiar and lovely ideal that is the English home in the countryside.

*E*nglish Country House Style is not solely the preserve of large country houses. Many of these stylistic shibboleths can be found in country cottages as well as stately homes. They speak of a grand but comfortable style of living. One that respects the past but whose formality is often pricked with contemporary flourishes and an eccentric English sense of fun. These design tropes all contribute to the fabulous interiors that English country houses are globally celebrated for. Houses which Evelyn Waugh once described as "our chief national artistic achievement."

Throughout this book, we refer to "the English." This is intended to be shorthand for "English countrymen and -women who choose to live in houses decorated in a classic English country house style" (which is obviously quite a mouthful). But of course, you don't need to be English to live in an English country house. And, indeed, your house doesn't need to be in England, or for that matter the countryside, for you to decorate it with an English country house look. Moreover, by writing about "the English" and the way they live, even with the above explanation of the shorthand, we will inevitably be making sweeping generalisations about behaviour, motivations, mores, and style. This book is intended to be a broad, subjective, and occasionally

> But of course, you don't need to be English to live in an English country house. And, indeed, your house doesn't need to be in England, or for that matter the countryside, for you to decorate it with an English country house look.

entertaining take on a certain decorative style and attitude. The brilliant interior designer Carlos Garcia is a case in point. Born and bred in Spain, Carlos fell in love with English country houses through the pages of *World of Interiors*. He is now a leading practitioner of the look that this book aims to describe and lives in a country house of his own in North Norfolk (included in these pages). When he first came to England, like many other budding decorators, he obsessively toured National Trust properties. "I fell in love with the country house look. And not just the style but the way of living. It's beautiful but pragmatic. European decoration is generally not about comfort, whereas English decoration is about comfort, layers, and respecting the past."

How can one describe this look? Not easily, because like charm itself, although instantly recognizable, it is hard to dissect. And part of the charm of English style is that it has no formal rules to be slavishly followed. It is a mixture of many things, and, indeed, blending things successfully together is one of its hallmarks. "It's a bit like mixing a salad," said Nancy Lancaster, who more than anyone else first codified the look. It is ironic that it took an American to show the English how their houses should be decorated. Nancy, who was born in Virginia at the turn of the twentieth century, lived in a succession of beautiful English houses. The way she decorated them was hugely influential, and through her purchase of Colefax and Fowler she commercialised the style. Nancy created rooms that were simultaneously elegant but informal and famously advocated that every room needed something ugly to stop it from becoming tiresome. "One needs light and shade because if every piece is perfect the room becomes a museum and lifeless."

Comfort is key. Lady Sibyl Colefax, who founded the eponymous firm that Nancy went on to buy, wrote, "The greatest mistake in the world is to believe that so-called good taste is any use without a sense of comfort to complete it."

Nostalgia is another trait. With old books, antique furniture, and inherited paintings, the English summon the spirits of the past. Lev Grossman, the American journalist, has written, "The paradox of the English country house is that its state of permanent decline, the fact that its heyday is always behind it, is part of the seduction." He is right, and English house decoration is often contrived to achieve this faded charm. The worst sin one could commit in decorating a room is to make it look newly decorated. You need to use well-worn rugs, sun-bleached tapestries, paint colours that look like faded versions of their original selves. Nancy herself talked of the importance of "pleasing decay." There is a romance to it. It is also part of

> How can one describe this look?
> Not easily, because like charm itself,
> although instantly recognizable,
> it is hard to dissect.

a broader English affectation—like self-deprecating humour and sporting amateurism—the desire not to be seen as trying too hard.

There's a tangible sense of life about an English country house. Partly because, like all living things, they evolve over time.

There's a tangible sense of life about an English country house. Partly because, like all living things, they evolve over time. But also because they are rarely tidy and never sterile. If you walked into a country house whose human residents had suddenly, magically, been spirited away, you would still sense their presence—in the freshly laid fire in the hall, the gently melting ice in the bucket on the drinks table, the smell of freshly cut flowers. And through the half-finished puzzle on the table in the library, the imprint of bottoms on squidgy sofas, the hiss of a kettle on the Aga top, and the stamped letters waiting for the postbox on the hall table. It is this vivacity that is so seductive about the country house.

In our own reverie, let us now walk up the gravelled drive of the ideal English country house, knock on its front door, and seek out its secrets.

Below: The kitchen at Southrop Manor. The cabinetry is painted in Edward Bulmer's Vert de Gris and the walls in Bulmer's Silver White.

Overleaf: Eighteenth-century Salthrop House in Wiltshire

1

The Entrance Hall

"You never get a second chance to make a first impression," goes the old maxim attributed to Oscar Wilde. And this is just as true for houses as it is for people. The entrance hall of a country house is a chance to dress to impress and sets the tone for the rest of the house.

Previous spread, left: Dilys the lurcher takes up position in the hallway of Waverton House in Gloucestershire.

Previous spread, right: The entrance hall of Briningham House in Norfolk, home to Sophie Crossley, is notable for its staircase, reputed to have come from Admiral Lord Nelson's London house. Jack the Labrador lies beneath a circular hall table that came from an antiques shop in nearby Holt called the Spotted Tiger.

Above: A view from the vestibule into the entrance hall of Bellamont House. Above the fireplace is an impressive display of talwar swords that celebrate Sir Eyre Coote's victory over the French at the Battle of Wandiwash in 1760.

Opposite: The late Anthony Syke's magnificent double-height entrance hall at Bellamont, the neo-Georgian house he created in Dorset

Τhe late architectural historian and property developer Anthony Sykes always maintained that the hall is one of the most important spaces in a house: "It is where the house introduces itself and looks you in the eye and says 'This is who I am.'" He believed that it should be impressive and somewhat dramatic, and that is exactly what he created in Bellamont House, the home in Dorset that he designed for his family thirty years ago. Anthony wanted to build a modern house along classical lines that would remind him of his childhood home, West Park in Hampshire, which sadly was demolished after the Second World War. Inspired by classical early-eighteenth-century architecture, he built a country house in Gothic revival style with an interior that subscribed

HENRY IV the KING of FRANCE and NAVARRE
1553-1610

to Palladian proportions. He designed the hall in the manner of William Kent but on a shrunken scale, to splendid effect. The double-height room is a cube, 24 feet high and 24 feet wide and overlooked by a balustraded gallery. It is cleverly colonnaded with two tiers of trompe l'oeil Corinthian pilasters and has deep arches leading off it to the rest of the house. In terms of decoration, Anthony conceived of the hall as a kind of Valhalla, or tribute to the exploits of his illustrious military forebears (including General Sir Eyre Coote), with various trophies, busts, and portraits. Most prominent, mounted over an original Georgian Portland stone chimneypiece, is a sunburst display of forty-six Talwar swords with a funeral hatchment (displaying a long-dead Coote's coat of arms) in the middle.

Of course, not every country house hall aspires to make such a grand statement, nor with such decorative exuberance, but most, one way or another, aim to impress their visitors and entice them to explore further into the house. Halls are often used to show off ancestral portraits, sporting trophies, coats of arms, banners, and, as with Anthony Sykes, militaria. They are also a chance, as Edward Bulmer puts it, "to show off your understanding of the language of classicism." Bulmer (who keeps a bust of Inigo Jones—"the father of classicism"—in his garden) is an historian and designer who has helped restore and decorate some of the greatest country houses in England. And in these grand residences, exterior and classical architectural features "somehow squeeze themselves through the front door." They are impressive but, in some ways, decoratively quite plain. That is because traditionally the hall would be a place of social mingling among the classes; tenants might be received here, the space would be shared by staff and family alike, and with all the comings and goings the footfall would be busier here than in any other part of the house. People entering the hall would bring with them the mud and dust (and horse manure) of the outside, so it made sense to have hard surfaces that could be easily cleaned, uncovered stone floors that could be swept and washed, and little or no upholstery. One generally furnishes a hall with chairs or settles for visitors to rest on or remove their boots, but these, for the reasons just described, would be of plain wood, uncovered by material. The tradition remains today, and most country houses will sport polished mahogany hall chairs. To the same end, in the eighteenth and nineteenth centuries, cheaper unpigmented paint would have been used (as one might want to repaint more regularly). So, what one ends up with are quite imposing yet practical spaces that are, as Bulmer puts it, "certainly starker than the areas of richness that close friends would go on to enjoy in the rooms beyond."

One near-ubiquitous feature is a black and white stone floor, sometimes in a chequerboard style but, even more elegantly (at least to this author's eye), in a formal design of pale limestone tiles teamed with small black cabochon

Opposite: A circular hall table at Warmwell House in Dorset

inserts in a diamond shape. A floor like this is a classic feature of Georgian hallways and one heartily copied by modern architects and decorators of country houses today.

A fireplace is important because, coming in from the cold, nothing is more welcoming than a blazing log. And a stick basket by the door is fairly universal. In it is a carefully curated selection of canes with beautifully carved handles, often in the shape of animal heads. (Occasionally you might discover a sword stick with a terrifying blade hidden in its shaft.)

A circular table is typical and highly practical—partly as a place to display trinkets, campaign medals, carved pieces of marble, and so on, but also for piling up geraniums, dumping hats, and, most important of all, keeping the visitors' book. Every country house, without exception, has a leatherbound book to record the names of overnight guests, embossed with gold letters spelling out the name of the house. There is some debate over what a guest should write in this. Age-old convention dictates that one should simply record one's name and date of stay (and possibly an abbreviated address). Comments were frowned upon as being unspeakably vulgar. But over time people have started to write witty poems, heartfelt thank-yous, or amusing anecdotes from the weekend, and even draw little illustrations. Staunch conservatives frown upon it, but recently *Tatler* magazine, arbiter of good taste, decreed that comments are now acceptable!

But come, let's leave such petty matters aside and, as honoured guests ourselves, pass through the entrance hall and on into the rest of the house to see what treasures lie beyond . . .

Above: The hall at Southrop Manor boasts an extraordinarily ancient twelfth-century Norman archway (that leads through to the dining room). The walls around it are painted with Farrow and Ball's India Yellow.

Opposite: The entrance hall of Warmwell House—a Jacobean manor in the heart of Hardy's Dorset. The stick basket and hunting boots are classic accoutrements of the English country house hall.

The Entrance Hall of the
Court of Noke, Edward
Bulmer's Queen Anne house
in Herefordshire

Opposite, above left: A pair of Biedermeier fan-shaped chairs on either side of a Dutch longcase clock in the hallway of Buscot Park in Oxfordshire

Opposite, above right: The entrance hall of Salthrop House

Opposite, below: The diamond-pattern wallpaper in this hall is by Blithfield and Company. In front of the old family rocking horse are a pair of otters peering out of the front door. The basket in the corner contains not only sticks, fishing rods, and a net but also a witch's broomstick left over from Halloween.

Right: A comical llama doorstop and a large collection of fluorescent heeled trainers bring a very English sense of levity to the grand furniture in this hallway in Devon.

Opposite: Interior designer Joanna Wood's manor house in the Cotswolds. The entrance hall was designed by local architects Johnston Cave with a Buscot stone floor. Impressive hunting trophies adorn the walls.

Left: Sitting on this walnut chest of drawers is a pair of palm lamps topped with shades from Pierre Frey.

Left: A giant log basket in the hall of art dealer Simon Dickinson's house in Gloucestershire, with an elegant "hang" of paintings behind

Opposite: An impressively filled stick basket carved from a tree trunk. The Shakespeare mask on the wall behind came from the legendary decorator Robert Kime and has an elaborate baroque scrollwork gilt frame.

2

The Boot Room

The boot room is arguably the most important
room in the house as it is where the dog sleeps.

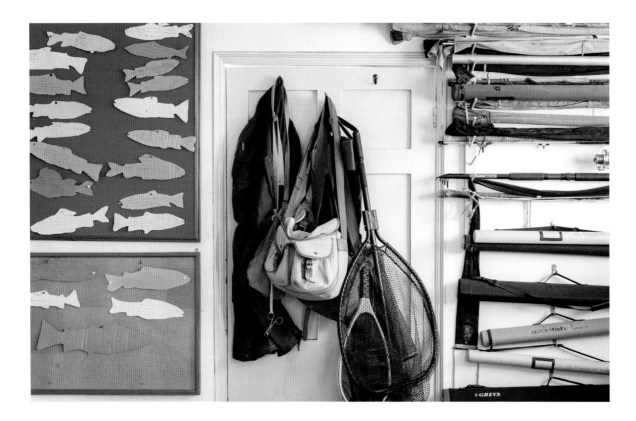

Previous spread, left: The settle in the boot room at the Court of Noke was built by Emma Bulmer's great-grandfather in a seventeenth-century style. The fabric is from Borderline (founded by Sally Baring). A bale of hats (the correct collective noun) sits on the shelf above.

Previous spread, right: Basil the basset hound and Dilys the lurcher, in their boot room. The wallpaper is by Pierre Frey.

Above: The boot room of a keen fisherman. The cardboard cutouts on the left commemorate notable first fish caught by various children over the years.

Opposite: Antler used as hat hooks in the Gloucestershire hallway of interior decorator Amanda Hornby.

A long with being the home of the family's most beloved member, the boot room's importance comes from being the gatehouse that prevents the mud, blood, feathers, and leaves of the English countryside from being transferred to the rest of the house.

"There is no such thing as bad weather, only the wrong clothes" is the mantra of the English country set, and here they lovingly store their Barbours, field coats, tweed jackets, and Wellington boots. Its walls are a shrine to country sports and hung with pony club rosettes, hunting prints, models of fish and mounted taxidermy in the form of game birds, fox masks, and stags' heads. Vital sporting equipment is artfully displayed (faux casually): fishing rods, shooting sticks, tennis racquets (including the occasional wooden one), riding crops, cartridge bags, lacrosse sticks, polo mallets, gun sleeves, cricket bats, and so on. There is also the paraphernalia of the equally important but more delicate outdoor pursuits of walking, gardening, and picnicking.

Most of all, there are hats. The English love their headgear, and every boot room worth its name will have an enormous collection of different hats often hanging from the antlers of the aforementioned taxidermy.

Hats have always been an English obsession, but their popularity has waned over the years, and the English country house remains its last great stronghold. Here you might find, for instance: the bowler hat, which prior to being adopted by city gents was originally commissioned by Edward Coke—nephew of the second Earl of Leicester—of Holkham Hall, who

The doorway into a boot room from a kitchen in Somerset. The pig is an old butcher's sign that the owner found in Kingsettle Antiques in Semley. The paisley circles wallpaper on the boot room wall is by Sanderson. The limestone floor in the foreground is from Artisans of Devises.

wanted a sturdy, close-fitting hat to protect his gamekeepers' heads from both poachers and low-hanging branches. Holkham gamekeepers still wear them on shoot days (as do some people for hunting). You might also find trilbies (which are most often worn racing, apart from at Ascot, where men wear silk top hats in the Royal Enclosure), and various sporting headgear, including riding hats with velvet covers, helmets for playing cricket and Panama hats for watching it, tweed caps for shooting, and deerstalkers.

But the boot room is also a repository for outdated, inherited head wear: pith helmets, straw boaters, army berets, cricket caps, guardsman's bearskins, 1920s ladies' cloches, and tasselled smoking caps. These are arranged prettily and only occasionally taken down, de-cobwebbed, and worn (mostly for fancy dress purposes). And one must not forget the head scarf, much loved by the late queen. These beautifully designed silk squares, made by the likes of Hermès, are kept in a special drawer along with kid leather gloves and cashmere wrist warmers.

A large, deep butler sink for washing small dogs, gutting fish, cleaning muddy footwear, cutting flowers, and rinsing garden vegetables is extremely

Above left: The magnificent carved oak panelling of Wolfeton Hall in Dorset dates back to the 1500s. A settle in the hall passage for removing one's boots sits below a portrait of Frances Weld, painted in around 1700.

Above right: This Charles Pollock bench is modern but with a vintage patina. Its cushion is covered in Vaison Bleu Anglais by Nicole Fabre. The walls are covered in an albaca material by Tatiana Tafur.

useful. Generously sized cupboards are key. Georgian-style "housekeeper" cupboards with drawers below are useful for the alarming amount of clobber that invariably collects in this area of the house.

A table (perhaps with a baize cloth) is important for gun cleaning, cricket bat oiling, and so on; and, if there is space, a campaign table in the middle of the room for laying out kit and studying maps for the next expedition one is planning is a wonderful thing.

A bench is absolutely vital to sit on when pulling on or off boots and shoes and removing wet socks. Balancing on one leg whilst attempting this—particularly after a certain age—is simply not on. It is also a place to sit and take a deep breath before braving the elements. Old church pews are perfect for this and can often be picked up cheaply at auctions along with tall antique settles of mahogany or oak. Alternatively, people are increasingly commissioning bespoke, built-in benches. Ideally, these are high enough to store Wellington boots or storage baskets underneath, with long rows of peg rails and hat shelves above.

In fact, contemporary boot rooms often boast exquisite cabinetry worthy of the smartest rooms in the house. Giving each family member their own section is practical and cuts down on the endless search through similarly hued dung-coloured coats to find your own.

Wallpaper is becoming more popular, as this is a functional room largely devoid of fabrics, and so decorative paper gives an opportunity to bring colour and interest.

Boot jacks are a must, and boot rooms are often home to a collection of wicker basketry. These range from picnic hampers (often from Fortnum & Mason) and willow gardening trugs to multi-sized baskets used as decorative storage for rugs, gloves, scarfs, and tennis balls. If the ancient flagstones of one's boot room preclude modern underfloor heating, then a raised dog bed to keep the treasured family pet off the chilly floor and away from drafts is vital.

Boot rooms have become more and more lusted over in recent years. Endless magazine articles are devoted to them, and you can find thousands of images of them on the likes of Pinterest and Instagram. People without them dream about the glorious practicality of owning a room where all the gear that clogs up their kitchens and hallways (and lives) can be safely contained in one space. But boot rooms also speak of pleasurable lives largely lived outdoors in the glorious English countryside. Who doesn't want to head outside with a gardening trowel/croquet mallet/fishing rod in one's hand or a picnic blanket under one's arm and a dog by one's side, wearing one's scruffiest clothes? Which brings us to a final decorative point: Boot rooms don't need mirrors in them. You shouldn't care how you look going out, and when you get back in, it's time for a bath anyway.

Opposite, above: Bespoke cabinetry, including a special alcove for hanging polo sticks

Opposite, below: An umbrella-cum-stick stand with a bench built around it, built by a local joiner to the owner's design. The cabinetry is painted with Tarlatan by Paint & Paper Library. The baskets are for hats, gloves, and shooting socks. The cat is called Uno, after the family's favourite card game.

Left: The boot room of a keen horsewoman. It has a reclaimed brick floor and tongue-and-groove panelling with a rail that is useful for hanging coats. The base of an old dresser is good for storing gloves and other bits, and its top is a useful surface for cleaning boots.

Opposite: The boot room at Bellamont House with its antler hatstand and church pew bench

Above: A wall of rosettes celebrating equestrian success in both dressage and eventing, mostly won on a hunter named Flashy (named after her beautiful flashing, dappled bottom).

Right: No country house worth its salt is without a croquet set. Jaques, a sports and games manufacturer founded in 1795, makes some of the finest equipment.

Opposite: The boot room at Briningham Hall was designed by Francis Keane of the architectural firm Haydon Finch. The bespoke panelling and cabinetry are painted in Little Greene's Normandy Grey. The limestone floor is Normandy Buff from Stamford Stone.

Above: Bespoke benching that is high enough to store tall Wellington boots underneath. A generous hat shelf big enough to accommodate, amongst other things, a taxidermy albino pheasant. And Oscar the cat, arguably the finest mouser in Gloucestershire, hidden amongst the coats.

Left: The interior decorator and designer Birdie Fortescue has a basket-filled boot room with a floor tiled with Norfolk Pamments.

3

The Aga

For non-afficionados, an Aga is a traditional cast-
iron oven with a brightly enamelled surface that sits,
permanently on, in the heart of every English country
house, and indeed in the heart of every Englishman
or -woman who grew up knowing one.

Previous spread, left:
Conker the spaniel assumes
her natural position in front
of the Aga in this Somerset
kitchen. Above her is a
drawing of a mackerel by
Jonathon Delafield Cook.
And on the shelf above that
is a collection of synthetic
crystal neon jugs by Mario
Luca Giusti.

Previous spread, right:
Carlos Garcia's whippets,
Theodora and Tristan,
take up their favourite
spot in front of the
Aga. Above the Aga is a
collection of eighteenth-
and nineteenth-century
Chinese porcelain created
for the English market.
Some old stilton pots from
Fortnum & Mason stand
behind the hot plate.

Above: A small Welsh
dresser from the early
seventeenth century with
Scottish spongeware on the
top shelf on either side of a
Staffordshire figure of the
Prince of Wales. A mixture
of eastern European
and French pottery sits
on the shelf below. The
Staffordshire hens are all
nineteenth century (and
the one in the middle was
part of a collection of John
Fowler's).

Opposite: One of Carlos's
chickens (a Sussex called
Sandra) making herself at
home in front of the butler
sink. Behind the taps are
a selection of Delft tiles,
some old, some new.

With a batch of scones in the top oven, a stew simmering away below, the kettle whistling on top, damp shooting socks drying on the rail, and a sleeping dog pressed against the warm base (making small, blissful whimpering sounds as he dreams of picking up partridges), the Aga is a happy thing indeed. It's where mothers lean to drink their coffee, crumpets are toasted in wire racks, and teenage broken hearts are mended. It's where bottles of wine are brought to stand and lose their cellar frigidity. The English love to tell stories of sodden orphaned lambs being carried in from the farm and brought back to life in the lowest warming oven (before, presumably, being roasted in the top oven a few months later). It is far more than just a cooker. It represents everything that is good about family life and home.

The Aga is so deeply buried into the English psyche that it has spawned a genre of popular fiction. The *Aga saga* is a term that has been incorporated

into the *Oxford Companion to Literature* since 2000. It refers to novels specifically set in the English countryside that combine family drama and illicit romance against a backdrop of flagstoned halls, Wellington boots, and cups of tea. Rachel Johnson (Boris's sister) wrote a hilarious one called *Shire Hell*. She once commented in the *Times*, "I don't think I've ever disliked anyone who owns an Aga. I'm afraid I have two. Both are cream."

Cream was the original shade and remains incredibly popular, but Agas today are available in a dazzling array of colours, and it is even possible to commission a bespoke enamel to match your favourite Farrow & Ball paint. In the first instance, they were coal-fired, and then more recently, fuelled with oil. But nowadays you can run them on practically anything. Electric Agas have become quite popular because they are quick and easy to turn on and off. But that rather misses the point. An Aga should always be on, pumping out heat and comfort even in midsummer. There is nothing more disappointing than walking into a kitchen, making a beeline for the Aga, and finding it cold to the touch. Edward Bulmer points out that "there is no good practical argument for an Aga but nothing else warms you up both physically and emotionally."

Like many English icons (tea, pheasants, St. George) the Aga didn't originate on these shores. It was invented in 1922 by the Nobel Prize–winning Swedish physicist Dr. Gustav Dalen (although he was a laureate for his work in illuminating lighthouses rather than warming English kitchens). But Agas have become as English as the ribs of beef roasted within them, and no country house is complete without one.

Of course, the Aga isn't the only motif of the English country house kitchen. We mustn't forget the dresser, the butler sink (with a view out to the garden), or the scrubbed oak table. The open-shelved kitchen dresser is a classic example of country house style being both pretty and practical. Dressers are lovely, principally for displaying the spongeware and pottery that the English love to collect. Open shelves for plates and glasses are the same; it is great to be able to find what you want easily, and they are so much more characterful than the stark closed cupboards of modern fitted kitchens. The English don't want to have to burrow around in dark cupboards to find their favourite mug, which, by the way, is made by Emma Bridgewater. Bridgewater mugs are iconic themselves. Made by the eponymous Staffordshire potter, these half-pint mugs are decorated with beautiful images created by Matthew Rice, often depicting the flora and fauna of the English countryside. Labradors are a particularly popular subject, as are the mugs that celebrate notable royal occasions—engagements, jubilees, and coronations.

Like many English icons (tea, pheasants, St. George) the Aga didn't originate on these shores.

Opposite: These chairs are covered in an old Colefax and Fowler material that came from a giant pair of curtains that the owner cut up. The doll's house was bought at Bonhams and was originally an Edwardian linen press. On the kitchen table are a pair of Staffordshire dogs, plus a pair of swans, "which are having a bit of a renaissance at the moment," says the owner, who is an avid collector of pottery. The spongeware teapot (next to a delicious orange and almond cake) is from Bell Pottery.

Above: The colour scheme of this Cotswolds kitchen was created by Vanessa Konig, who both consults on colour and has a huge range of her own beautiful paints (Konig Colours). The bird print on the wall is of Guatemalan quetzals. The teapot and mugs on the pine kitchen table are by Emma Bridgewater. Oscar the tabby cat sits at the head.

Opposite: This Norfolk kitchen was designed by Martin Moore. The oversized pendant lights come from Hector Finch. The kitchen stools are from Neptune. The marble behind the light blue Aga comes from Calcutta. The wreath of dried flowers was created by the owner herself.

All good kitchens have a door leading out to the garden. The English take the sport of gardening very seriously indeed, so much so that keen gardeners compete for gold medals at the Chelsea Flower Show every year. King Charles III is as green-fingered as his subjects, believing like Sir Thomas More that "the soul cannot thrive in the absence of a garden." The English love their deep, herbaceous borders filled with delphiniums, foxgloves, and hollyhocks; their formal lawns; their rose gardens; their topiary; and their wall-climbing clematis, honeysuckle, and wisteria. But it is the kitchen garden that reigns supreme. Home-grown garden produce is the key to successful country living, and a typical kitchen will be filled with freshly picked or dug fruit and vegetables—lots of which will find its way, via the Aga, into jars on the kitchen dresser in the form of crab-apple jelly, raspberry jam, pickled marrow, and other delicious condiments. Sloe and damson gin is a particular fetish of the English, and early autumn finds kitchen tables across the country littered with fruit to be pricked and placed into Kilner jars where they are steeped with alcohol. Can there be a more bucolic pastime than to sit in such a kitchen, warmed by the Aga, as the days start to shorten and the first frost beckons?

Above: Another dog hogging the warmest spot in the house. This time it's Mulan, a Staffordshire bull terrier crossed with a boxer, on a smart tapestry bed. Above the black Aga are hand-painted tiles from Fired Earth with images of different English trees.

Right: The kitchen table at Southrop Manor covered in a cloth designed by the house's owner, Caryn Hibbert. Caryn, along with running Thyme (a country house hotel and estate in the Cotswolds), produces exquisite fabrics and other products inspired by nature through Bertioli, a company she runs with her daughter Milly.

Above: A large, handsome dresser in the kitchen at Bellamont. Nancy Lancaster always maintained that oversized scale was much better than undersized.

Opposite: A classic black Aga with an ingenious bracketed pot-filler tap above

Left: These open shelves above the kitchen sink were designed by the owner, who says, "It's so useful to have glasses right above where you want them" (alongside teapots and cow creamers). Behind the original Shaws butler sink are some Bell Pottery jugs and a Staffordshire figure of the famous highwayman Dick Turpin. Pretty floral curtains hide cleaning products on the open shelves below.

Opposite: Brightly coloured enamel Le Creuset casseroles sit next to a fashionably white Aga. The owner considered a cream one, "but it was just that bit too creamy." The dog is called Dolly "after Dolly mixture sweets because she is such a mix herself. Mostly cocker spaniel and beagle, but really just a mongrel."

A beautiful contemporary country house kitchen designed by Emma Sims-Hilditch

4

The Dining Room

In a world that has almost universally embraced eat-in kitchens and open-plan living, the English country house is one of the last bastions of the formal dining room.

Previous spread, left: The dining room at Southrop Manor. The tablecloth is a Bertioli design (Cherry Blossom) by the house's owner, Caryn Hibbert.

Previous spread, right: The dining room at Warmwell House in Dorset. The table, which can be extended to seat twenty-four people, is surrounded by fabric-covered early Georgian chairs. At the end of the room are a pair of Chippendale mirrors and in between them a portrait of "Miss Sambrook"—ancestor and namesake of the current owner.

Above: The dining room at Castle Hill house in Devon, home of the Fortescue family since 1684. The table seats twenty.

Opposite: The octagonal canopied dining room at Bellamont whose owner, Anthony Sykes, designed it to look like a campaign tent. The fabric is a simple ticking found in Bridport Market.

Whether vast in scale with many-leafed tables that can seat twenty-four (or more), or an intimate space for dinner parties of six, a room dedicated to the purpose is where the English country set like to eat. These rooms are dominated by silverware, mahogany furniture, candlelight, rich colour schemes, and luxurious wallpapers, sideboards from which guests serve themselves, and ancestral portraits—because the English love to dine beneath the unblinking stares of their forebears (and also remind their guests of their noble lineage).

Dorothy Parker once described the dinner party as "the lowest form of taking nourishment." And it is true that the very thought of such formal dining can cause some people to break out in hives. Television chefs and social commentators alike advocate small, single-course, relaxed "kitchen suppers" as the ideal way to entertain. Yet surely there is something to be said, when the occasion suggests, for escaping from the bustle, noise, and distractions of the kitchen for something a bit more special?

The English believe in the importance of a separate room so you can focus on conviviality and conversation. A beautiful dining room should stimulate the senses and completely transport you from the everyday, providing the ultimate interactive human experience.

Sometimes people wrongly associate the dining room with unpleasantly formal "events" that they might have experienced. Whereas the true purpose of the country house dining room is to put guests at their ease. The ultimate aim is for them to feel celebratory and relaxed, not over-awed.

Whereas the true purpose of the country house dining room is to put guests at their ease. The ultimate aim is for them to feel celebratory and relaxed, not over-awed.

Sir Winston Churchill used his dining room at Chartwell, his country house in Kent, to entertain close friends and family, as well as to host lunches and dinners for some of the biggest names of the twentieth century. He used a large, circular dining table, which he thought to be the most sociable shape, and to go around it he commissioned a set of supremely comfortable, sprung-seated armchairs. They were designed especially for the Churchills by the architect Phillip Tilden and covered in an arum lily design, which complemented the vivid green curtains of the room. Tilden's sole aim was to create an air of affability.

The interior decorator Carlos Garcia's dining room shares this aim. Upholstered chairs (covered in a Robert Kime fabric), a roaring fire, and a large seventeenth-century tapestry cloaking one wall create a cocooning sense of comfort. Carlos is also a great believer in candlelight. "When we dine in here, the room is entirely lit by candles. Candlelight is both flattering and romantic." Adding to the romance of the room is Carlos's exceptionally pretty Royal Crown Derby dinner service with a pattern called "Olde Avesbury" illustrating exotic love birds.

A beautiful dining room is all in the details, and everything should be designed to delight the senses. Crockery is important. Pretty plates should take precedence over the everyday utilitarian ones used in the kitchen. Bespoke services are often used. Some people have their family crest embossed on their tableware; the artist Phoebe Dickinson has designed

Above: A circular dining room table at Blickling Lodge in Norfolk. The room was decorated by Birdie Fortescue with tobacco-coloured grasscloth walls.

Opposite: The original eighteenth-century panelling of Carlos Garcia's house in Norfolk is painted Parma Gray by Farrow & Ball. Sitting on the mantelpiece is a Spode dining platter. The room is lit exclusively by candles.

her own plates with a giraffe motif to reference her husband's nickname; and a peer of my acquaintance has commissioned several dinner services, each one reflecting a different order he carries (The Most Excellent Order of the British Empire, The Royal Victorian Order, etc.).

Silver centrepieces are typical. Alongside candelabras and epergnes, models of pheasants and other gamebirds are popular. Laura Duckworth-Chad, at Castle Hill in Devon, has a silver figure on horseback in the centre of her table. It is a model of a cavalry officer from the Royal Scots Greys, presented to her forebear Captain Viscount Ebrington on the occasion of his marriage by his fellow officers.

Traditionally, guests are invited to serve themselves from a sideboard (or in very grand houses from a butler holding a tray). Often you will find dishes on a Wembury Warmer—a traditional steel hot plate with elegant little claw feet. Much like the drawing room drinks table, it is generous-spirited to let guests pick and choose what, and how much, they want to eat. But close relations must remember the golden rule: FHB—Family Hold Back (i.e., the youngest son of the house shouldn't pile his plate high with chicken breast, leaving a withered wing to the invited guest behind him).

The dining room used to double up as a smoking room, and it became a tradition for ladies to withdraw post-dinner, leaving the gentlemen to their port and cigars. Such nonsense is long abolished, but a recent article in *Tatler* magazine advises the modern hostess to "turn the patriarchy on its head by sending the men to the drawing room and sitting round the table with the women to drink, smoke, and talk about shagging."

Even its most ardent advocates would concede that the dining room is not for everyday use. Recurring cartoons have often poked fun at the idea of a married couple formally dining alone at either end of a long table and having to shout to one another before the husband trudges the length of the room to pass the salt.

My day job is finding country houses for my clients to buy. Recently, I took a couple in their forties around a beautiful Georgian house in the Cotswolds. We walked into the darkened dining room.

"Oh dear," said the man, "we will have to work out what to do with this."

"Why?" I asked.

"No one uses dining rooms anymore. When would we be in here? Only on the rare occasion all our friends are down, or for family stuff at Christmas and Easter."

"So only on the most important and joy-filled moments of your year, then?" We both paused, and for a brief, wistful moment, the room came alive as we imagined the laughter and the candlelight and the tinkle of crystal glasses.

Opposite: The artist Phoebe Dickinson's dining room in Gloucestershire. The main picture is by the early twentieth-century English artist Fred Elwell, who painted lots of interiors. The pictures of peppers, oranges, and lemons are by Diarmuid Kelley, an artist friend of Phoebe's. On the sideboard is a Wembury Warmer—a traditional steel hot plate.

Above: An example of dining-room-table silverware at Castle Hill

Right: The vibrant green colour of this room was based on Rhoda Birley's dining room at Charleston Manor in East Sussex (Rhoda was the grandmother of Robin Birley, the owner of 5 Hertford Street, where a picture of this dining room hangs).

Above the fireplace is a portrait of the owner by Pietro Annigone (who was famous for his portraits of Queen Elizabeth II).

This exceptionally pretty
breakfast-cum-dining room
has bespoke wallpaper made
by Allyson McDermott. The
chairs came from Piers Pisani
Antiques, and the mirror is
from Brownrigg, which is
run by the wonderful Jorge
Perez-Martin.

Above: This tiny dining room in the Cotswolds, decorated by Octavia Dickinson, seats a maximum of six people (which many argue is the perfect number for dinner). It is painted Print Room Yellow by Farrow & Ball, a colour which works well as a backdrop for black-and-white prints—in this case, of the owner's ancestors.

Right: An unusual elliptical boardroom table fits this dining room perfectly and makes group conversation much easier than a traditional rectangle. The porcelain Famille Rose plates on the wall were bought from Christie's. The panelled wall itself is painted in Julie's Dream by Little Greene.

A formal dining hall in a grand
country house in Oxfordshire

5

The Downstairs Loo

The downstairs loo is a country house classic and often the most highly decorated room in the house, with elaborate wallpapers and sometimes even trompe l'oeils. The walls of this room, more than just a "temple of convenience," are often a shrine to family history and achievements, festooned with school photos, army commissions, family trees, team insignia, and mementos.

Previous spread, left: Edward Bulmer's downstairs loo at his country house in Herefordshire. The loo furniture is an "incontinence chair" from an antiques shop in Hereford and originally would have just had a chamber pot in it. The walls are covered in a Rubelli fabric.

Previous spread, right: A good range of classic "loo books," including cartoons; tomes on shooting, gardens, dogs, and birdlife; and a collection of humorous quotations from His Late Royal Highness The Duke of Edinburgh.

Above: A pig-themed loo in Dorset, including a ceramic Wemyss Ware pig on the lavatory bench

Downstairs loos are inevitably quite masculine rooms, not least because the country house husband often finds himself banned from the marital bathroom lest he defile its pretty and fragrant nature. And it is a place his wife generally chooses to avoid, thereby giving him a free hand to display random relics (often of a military nature), hang cartoons of questionable taste, and, most importantly, surround the lavatorial throne with books of his choosing—some of which might display a "boyish" (i.e., puerile) sense of humour. Having said that, one shouldn't generalise, and some cloakrooms are paeons of good taste whose shelves are thoughtfully filled with volumes of poetry and works of great writers.

In a letter to his son in the mid-eighteenth century, Lord Chesterton advocated reading on the loo and told the story of an acquaintance who liked to enjoy Latin poetry when on the lavatorial throne. The man in question would buy a cheap edition of, say, Ovid's poems, tear out a couple of sheets, and take them with him to the "necessary place." There he would then enjoy reading them before putting them to further practical use and flushing them away "as a sacrifice to cloacina."

In the era of super-soft Andrex loo paper (whose advertisements famously feature a Labrador dog—the English country house set's most favoured breed), there is no need to destroy the books in the downstairs loo. Thank goodness, because the "loo book" is a precious genre and there are works of wonder to be found there. People popping in for a quick pee can easily find themselves distracted for quite some time (leading hosts to sometimes wonder, "Do you think she's fallen down it?!").

Books or passages of books that can be read in one, quite literal, sitting are obviously sensible. Reference books, miscellanies, and compendiums all abound. Humorous books are favoured with Private Eye annuals, Victoria Mather's *Social Sterotypes*, and Stephen Potter's *One-Upmanship* all commonly found. But the sine qua non of all lavatorial libraries is the late John Julius Norwich's *Christmas Crackers*. For nearly fifty years, the 2nd Viscount Norwich kept a commonplace book, which he distilled into a slim pamphlet, that he would produce annually, initially for friends and eventually for a grateful public. In it, he recorded all the favourite things that he came across that year. These wonderfully eclectic collations include quotes, poems,

Above left: No "loobrary" is complete without John Julius Norwich's *Christmas Crackers*.

Above right: A small portrait of a foxhound above the loo, and more humorous books, including the 1980s classic *The Official Sloane Ranger Handbook*

diary entries, inscriptions on gravestones, ridiculous newspaper articles, and so on. Utterly brilliant and eminently re-readable.

In terms of lavatorial equipment itself, the English favour old-fashioned loos. Edward Bulmer, the architectural historian, is a great fan. "I'm always amused by old thunder boxes and night cupboards for chamber pots, but we have some friends who think they are terribly unsanitary." But it is the original loo, invented by the brilliantly named Thomas Crapper, with an elevated cistern operated by the pull of a chain, that remains most sought after.

> In terms of lavatorial equipment itself, the English favour old-fashioned loos.

Downstairs loos are often quite show-offy with old school photographs proving you went somewhere smart, old team photos to remind yourself and guests that you were once young and sporty, photos of yourself hunting or skiing or standing on the wings of a bi-plane (!) to show your daring nature. The room is often an offshoot of the boot room, and so cartridge bags, walking sticks, and cricket bats might find themselves in there.

Cartoons are popular—antique prints from *Punch* magazine or the work of modern newspaper satirists. Caricatures related to hunting and shooting by the likes of the late Bryn Parry are popular. Press clippings related to the house's owners, particularly if they are negative (as the English are a self-deprecating lot) also abound. Quite often you will find framed poems or illustrations, or amusing thank-you letters written by friends.

Also on the walls you might see local maps, pictures of old houses, family trees, and collages of photographs recording holidays. In some ways this is less a cloakroom than a family archive. As a visitor to a country house, if you want to quickly get to grips with who your hosts are and what drives them emotionally, a quick five minutes spent examining the walls of their downstairs loo will tell you far more about both their heritage and their inner life than hours spent in their company in the drawing room. Which I suppose is rather the point.

Opposite: Family memorabilia, drawings, handmade cartoons, school photos, certificates, poems, pictures of old houses, holiday photos—an archetypal English downstairs loo.

Above: A mildly salacious, horse-themed cartoon by Mark Huskinson—typical of downstairs loo humour

Left: A modern lavatory disguised in an antique chamber pot cabinet

Opposite: Another antique chamber pot "throne" with modern-day plumbing. The walls are covered in a typical fashion with framed family photographs and equestrian memorabilia.

Opposite: A bespoke washstand created from a sink and marble top (both from a reclamation yard near Exeter) on a wooden structure designed so its owner—who is six foot five—doesn't have to bend to wash his hands. A bugle sits on top, "for sounding the all clear," and underneath, a collection of leather cartridge bags.

Above left: A classically masculine downstairs loo in Somerset. School photographs, cricket bat, shooting stick, and a proper loo library. The Boxing Hares wallpaper is by Barneby Gates.

Above right: Leather gun slips hanging on the back of the loo door. Original "BB" scraperboard illustrations hang on the left. These hugely evocative images by Denys Watkins-Pitchford describing country life are highly collectible.

Left: A grand cloakroom in Gloucestershire, designed by Leonora Birts, with glamorous wallpaper and a traditional washstand. The paper is called Marbleized Velvet by Beata Heuman.

Opposite: A fabulous picture wall in Sophie Conran's downstairs loo in Wiltshire. The fuchsia flock wallpaper she designed herself in collaboration with Art House.

Overleaf: Lady Delia Goodenough's spectacular loo at Beck Hall in Norfolk. The tiger whose skin is on the floor was shot by a Victorian forebear.

Left: Checkerboard tiles and Pink Ground Farrow & Ball walls in this lavatory in Gloucestershire. Military memorabilia on the walls and, as ever, plenty of books

Opposite: A vibrantly coloured loo with hunting print curtains and plenty of shelving for essential reading material

6

The Fireplace

Whether you believe that Prometheus stole it from the gods or not, there is evidence to suggest that humans first started using fires in a controlled way up to one million years ago. They are, as the architectural historian Edward Bulmer puts it, "the oldest feature of human dwellings," and our cave-lurking ancestors took to them heartily.

T he fireplace's earliest use was for scaring off woolly mammals at night (and for barbequing them during the day). But as the millennia passed, it took on its more familiar guise as a place where humans would gather—and not just to cook or warm themselves, but to socialise.

The fireplace is the social centrepiece of every country house drawing room. This is where family and guests gather to gossip, warm their bottoms, and perform (often in the form of charades). Because it is the literal focal point of the room, all furniture is arranged to face it. Country house decoration starts at the fireplace and works its way out.

The chimneypiece (also known as a fire surround or mantelpiece) is often a work of art in itself. Fireplaces are really just openings in the bottom of the chimney stack, but they need to be dressed in fireproof materials like stone and marble and presented a chance for the architect to really make his mark. Beautiful antique fireplaces are much sought after today as salvage pieces. You can find them at reclamation yards or at a specialist firm like Jamb, which is famous for selling not only antiques but also its own beautiful reproductions.

Most country house fireplaces were built in an era when wood would be brought into the room, as required, by servants. In our more frugal and egalitarian times, we use log baskets made of wicker, which are kept next to

or near the fire. Phoebe Dickinson, the artist, when decorating her drawing room in Gloucestershire, commissioned a pair of bespoke baskets made to perfectly fit under the two bay windows of the room. They came from Coates English Willow, who, with nice symmetry, also make the charcoal sticks she uses for drawing. Other essential kit includes fire irons (poker, shovel, and tongs), a pair of bellows, boxes of kindling, toasting forks (for crumpets), and piles of old newspapers for lighting (the pink *Financial Times* is the prettiest). Instead of using matches, some people light their fires with an ingenious device called a Grenadier. It blows alarmingly hot air at the wood until it spontaneously combusts.

A brass fender around the hearthstone keeps ash in place and prevents flaming logs from rolling onto the carpet. Likewise, a spark guard is an essential piece of kit to prevent crackling wood spitting flammable embers onto your sofa. These meshes can be antique or modern, and folding or static screens. An old-fashioned but rather smart alternative is a chain-mail curtain within the fireplace itself that can be pulled across. You might sometimes see decorative fire screens, often of tapestry, but these are less about fire safety and were originally used to protect ladies' made-up faces from melting in the direct heat.

In the Georgian age, the mantel shelf on top of the fireplace was decorated with quite formulaic garniture. Symmetry was key. There would typically be three on the lintel, one above each jamb, and one in the middle. Most commonly, the objects would be baluster jars from China, urns, or obelisks. Nowadays these shelves are much more cluttered, although a general symmetry is appreciated. There is quite often a clock as a centrepiece, or perhaps a small piece of sculpture. Candlesticks or lamps are prevalent at either end, although lamps present a bit of a problem because of their trailing wires. However, with the development of long-lasting rechargeable batteries, one can now find good-quality cordless lamps (the lighting company Pooky, based in Chelsea and the Cotswolds, has a good range).

In between, you might find little objets d'art, shells, feathers, pieces of children's art, and, of course, matches. Antique ribbed-glass match strikers with silver cuffs are much prized and highly collectible. A more modern version is glass bottles of long matches with brightly coloured tips, which are a staple of Christmas fairs. Pairs of Staffordshire dogs are popular. Carlos Garcia is particularly fond of them. "I love their perpetually surprised looks. Some people consider them quite garish, but I think they are charming and fun and deformalize things. They are beautifully ugly."

Finally, mantelpieces are used for displaying "stiffies"—invitations to smart parties and weddings on thick pieces of card engraved with copper-plate script. Plus, Christmas cards from royals, game cards from shoots, and so forth. They are indicators of one's social status and popularity, and

A sitting room decorated by Emma Sims-Hilditch with a large ottoman in front of the fire upholstered in a fabric from Christian Lee

dismaying to guests who inevitably notice them when standing by the fire and think, "Why wasn't I invited to that?!"

Above the fireplace, people choose between options of an overmantel mirror (whose base sits on the lintel) or a prominent picture, usually with a carved gilt frame. On either side there could be sconces or smaller pictures hanging in vertical lines.

But the most iconic accoutrement to a drawing room fireplace is the club fender. These padded seats on brass legs which surround the fire allow you to sit close, warming your backside, as you drink and chat. They are a clever way of introducing extra seating to the room without taking up too much space. They are also decorative in themselves and present a chance to experiment with relatively small pieces of fabulous fabric that one might be too shy to cover an entire sofa in. Sometimes they are break-fronted and effectively divided into two, and sometimes the seat goes all the way across. Norfolk-based interior designer Birdie Fortescue prefers the latter: "More room for more bums to sit on!"

The alternative to the club fender is to have a pair of small chairs. Carlos Garcia prefers this and uses antique nursing chairs. "You can linger for longer on a nursing chair. You can only perch on a fender for an hour or so having a drink—any longer is impossible, so a chair is more hospitable."

Hospitality is very much the point. "We no longer build fireplaces for warmth. We build them for the warmth of the soul; we build them to dream by, to hope by, to home by." The author of these words (Edna Ferber) is American, but the sentiment is very much shared by the English.

The fireplace in the library at Came House in Dorset—a Palladian country house built in 1754. William Morris Bird and Anemone wallpaper. The pineapple lamps on stands on either side of the fireplace are a typical country house motif. The pineapple is traditionally a symbol of hospitality and welcome.

Above: A French mirror sits on a pleasingly crowded mantel shelf, featuring (amongst other things) a handsome clock, a pair of porcelain pugs, and two angels "which went up one Christmas and we never got round to taking down," says the owner. A nursing chair sits in front.

Right: A pair of antique bellows at Wolfeton, a sixteenth-century manor house in Dorset

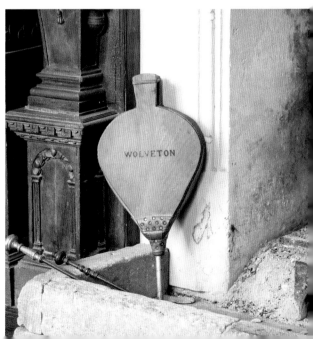

Clemmie Fraser's drawing room at Waverton—the house built by her grandfather in 1978 and designed by architect Quinlan Terry in a classical eighteenth-century style. In front of the fire is a horsehair-covered club fender.

Birdie Fortescue's sitting room in Norfolk. The sofa and armchair are covered in a Colefax and Fowler floral on linen with a bullion fringe. An antique rug sits on top of some sisal matting with a trim. Birdie prefers a club fender whose seat continues all the way across, as it gives "more room for more bums to sit on."

Opposite, above: An eighteenth-century mirror from Adam Calvert Bentley hangs above the fire in Carlos Garcia's sitting room. On the mantel shelf below, flanking a gilt clock, are a pair of early nineteenth-century polychrome Delft tiles featuring pomegranates. Also on the shelf are a pair of Staffordshire dogs.

Opposite, below: This sitting room belongs to the interior designer Leonora Birts, whose contemporary take on English country house style is much sought after. The club fender is from Acres Farm (the bespoke fender specialists) and is covered in an electric-blue horsehair fabric from John Boyd. On the mantelpiece are a pair of blue William Yeoward vases. The framed picture in the middle is a lithograph of the original sheet music for the Beatles' song "Yesterday," signed by its producer, George Martin. The gold candle sconces are from Jess Wheeler.

Left: The sitting room of Alexander Hope's Cotswold cottage, which was decorated with the help of interior designer Octavia Dickinson. The picture on the left is a late eighteenth-century allegorical depiction of Hope. The picture in the centre is a watercolour by Hugh Buchanan depicting the red drawing room at Hopetoun (arguably Scotland's finest stately home). Alexander put in the Arts and Crafts–style fireplace with William Morris tiles.

Left: The picture above this fireplace is a nineteenth-century French study of girls working on a fruit stall in an elaborately carved nineteenth-century frame from the Howell Collection.

The club fender is covered in a checkerboard stripe fabric by Pierre Frey Le Manach called Alesia.

Opposite: A black marble fireplace in Edward Bulmer's hall using a scagliola technique, whereby an outline is incised, then filled with pigmented plaster lime and made to look like marble. Bulmer designed it and commissioned artist Tom Kennedy to create it. It represents animal life in the nearby river—an otter on one jamb, an eel on another, plus a kingfisher, a dipper, a native crayfish, a brown trout, and a grayling.

7
Books

The country house library is a place of wonder. It can range in scale from a double-height behemoth with upper gallery, moveable ladders on casters, and a full-time archivist, right down to the shelved corner of a country cottage with a single feather-stuffed armchair providing a cosy nook for both reading and dozing.

Whether great or small, all English country house libraries subscribe to the immortal maxim that "books do furnish a room." This phrase was first coined by Anthony Bagshawe, a character in Anthony Powell's *A Dance to the Music of Time*. In fact, it was the title of the tenth book of Powell's twelve-volume series of novels describing the culture and manners of mid-twentieth-century England. And Bagshawe was right. Books do furnish a room, or certainly that is the belief of all English country house owners. They bring warmth, depth, colour and texture to a room. And that is just in terms of decoration. More importantly, they bring joy, learning, and endless diversion. The English consider a room without books to be soulless.

There are different ways to fit out a library. Some people opt for free-standing bookcases with classical pediments, while others prefer

ranks of bespoke bookshelves fitted to the room, or a hybrid of the two. Floor-to-ceiling cases should have graduated shelves of different heights accommodating taller books at ground level and shorter volumes at the top. Lighting is important. Moveable "library lights" on swinging arms that can be adjusted to illuminate different sections of books are useful. Shelves that run above doors are wonderful, or, best of all, book-filled shelves that cover the doors themselves, creating a secret jib that, when closed, creates quiet and privacy and a sense of being enveloped by literature.

Book are generally organised thematically—novels in one bookcase, biographies in another, and so forth. And serious bibliophiles, within these sections, will then arrange them alphabetically. But often arrangements are haphazard. Some people will loosely arrange books by colour. The artist Phoebe Dickinson likes to remove the dust jackets from modern novels because she finds the profusion of colours and imagery too garish and confused in a giant group. Freddie Cartwright, whose library in Somerset features in these pages, goes a different route. He collects scruffy first editions of all his favourite books and has them uniformly rebound in fine Moroccan leather and embossed with his crest so that one day his descendants will inherit a smart collection of all the books he loves. Speaking of leather-bound books, a ubiquitous country house library motif is the old-fashioned, large-format photo album. They are a labour of love to fill but wonderful to hold and behold, and infinitely superior to keeping digital images on a tablet.

The love of books spills out beyond the library itself, and books are used to furnish pretty much any room in the English country house. You will find them in bedrooms, where they are piled high on bedside tables and in pretty, waist-high bookcases. The mark of a good host is to make sure that one's weekend guests always have something stimulating to read. The mark of a superlative host is to pick books that might be particularly relevant or interesting to individual guests coming to stay. Things that people can dip into without having to finish make obvious sense. Diaries and memoirs, books of verse and collections of short stories, compendiums of passages from loved novelists distilled into single volumes (P. G. Wodehouse is, as always, particularly popular), travel writing, and best-of collections from newspaper columnists (like the late, great AA Gill) are all good ideas. Plus, something salacious and purposefully outrageous, like the novels of the Marquis de Sade or *50 Shades of Grey*. Newly released novels are well received but hard to finish in only a couple of days so they run the risk of being pinched at the end of the weekend.

Kitchens are also well stocked with books. Cookbooks, most obviously, with an emphasis on classic British writers like Elizabeth David, Hugh

> The love of books spills out beyond the library itself, and books are used to furnish pretty much any room in the English country house.

Opposite: Phoebe Dickinson's bookshelves in Gloucestershire. The painting of peaches is by her artist friend Diarmuid Kelley.

Fearnley-Whittingstall, Clare Macdonald, Simon Hopkinson, and Prue Leith. But also modern young writers like Skye McAlpine, Valentine Warner, and Amber Guinness. Here you will also find books on wine and more general books of food writing by the likes of William Sitwell and Tom Parker-Bowles.

Bathrooms are not exempt from the book craze. Here you will generally find a shelf of well-steamed paperbacks or, as in the case of Clemmie Fraser's bathroom in Gloucestershire, a large and fully stocked bookcase, for there is no greater pleasure than reading in the bath. And downstairs loos are often as well packed as libraries themselves. In fact, one country house owner describes hers as the "loobrary." Here you will find humorous tomes as mentioned in our chapter on cloakrooms.

And what books might you find in the actual country house library? Collections, obviously, are as eclectic as their owners, but there are some subjects and writers that seem perennially popular. In our snoopings across England for this book, we noted various books that seem inevitably to be on the shelves: the political diaries of Chips Channon and Alan Clarke; the novels of P. G. Wodehouse, Evelyn Waugh, Agatha Christie, and Nancy Mitford; Sir Walter Scott's Waverley novels, bound copies of *Punch* magazine, the historic naval dramas of Patrick O'Brian, and the Flashman novels of George Macdonald Fraser; Jilly Cooper; anything by or about Sir Winston Churchill; Burke's Peerage; the works of modern British historians like Niall Ferguson, Simon Schama, and Andrew Roberts; books on field sports (Earl Grey on fishing), naturalists like "BB" (the pseudonym for Denys Watkins-Pitchford) alongside modern nature writers such as Robert Macfarlane; endless reference books, particularly on gardens; Pevsner's survey of historic houses; Wisden's cricketing annuals.

If you were to build a country house library from scratch, you might start with some of the above. Even better, you would use the assistance of arguably London's finest bookshop, Heywood Hill. Founded in the 1930s on Curzon Street in Mayfair, this small but magnificent bookshop has an illustrious history. It was known to be the late queen's favourite bookshop and during the 1940s was partly run by Nancy Mitford. It was later bought by her brother-in-law the Duke of Devonshire, whose family still own and run it to this day. Heywood Hill offer a specialist service in assembling and delivering bespoke libraries to their customers. "Fill my library for me! These are my interests . . ." is all you need to say. And if they were to create an archetypal country house library, they might well include the works of that great novelist Jane Austen, whose books are peerless in their depiction of early nineteenth-century country house life. As she herself wrote in *Pride and Prejudice*, "I declare after all there is no enjoyment like reading! How much sooner one tires of anything than of a book! When I have a house of my own, I shall be miserable if I have not an excellent library."

Opposite: Clemmie Fraser's bathroom in Gloucestershire is this author's dream: thick carpet with rugs on top, pretty wallpaper, a huge bookcase crammed with interesting tomes and, best of all, a dog bed—so you have company as you read in the tub.

Above: A fabulous breakfront library bookcase in Somerset designed by its owner. It has slots in its base specifically designed for photograph albums and board games.

Opposite: The country house architect Christian Fleming's own library in Gloucestershire. The room is painted Farrow and Ball French Grey. The library lights come from Limehouse lighting. The sofa was made by interior designer Chloe Vestey with a Pierre Frey weave fabric.

Opposite: The library at Castle Hill in Devon. This room was rebuilt after a devastating fire in 1934.

Left: Books are piled everywhere in James Mackie's cottage in the Cotswolds and are a form of decoration in themselves.

A fine bookcase in the drawing room of this old rectory in Norfolk, incorporating a bust of Admiral Lord Nelson. Next to the bookcase is a print by the abstract artist Victor Passmore.

Above: Baloo, a Sandringham Labrador from a strain first bred by King George V, lies in front of an early nineteenth-century French bookcase in this library in Gloucestershire.

Opposite: A corner of a library belonging to the historian John Campbell. Campbell (author of the definitive biography of the early twentieth-century statesman Viscount Haldane) designed the bookcases himself. In front is a George III mahogany reading table with an Arts and Crafts chair.

Overleaf: A bookcase in the drawing room of Waverton House in Gloucestershire. The room is painted in Farrow & Ball's Light Blue.

8

The Drinks Table

No country house drawing room is complete without
a lavishly stocked and elegantly laid-out drinks table,
from which guests can help themselves.

Previous spread, left: A drawing room drinks table in Gloucestershire in front of a large family portrait by Victorian society painter Charles Furse. The little girl appears to have her hand in the ice bucket!

Previous spread, right: A drinks table is not just functional; the crystal and silver and jewel-coloured glass of the bottles makes for a fabulously decorative corner of a room.

Above: Classic cocktails like the dry martini reign supreme at the country house drinks table. And when it comes to martinis, the drier the better. Some people like a Montgomery, named after the famous field marshal who, it is said, liked the gin in his martini to overwhelm the vermouth in roughly the same ratio as he liked to outnumber his opponents in battle (fifteen to one). Others go further and only allow the shadow of the vermouth bottle to fall across their martini glass.

Opposite: In this drawing room, an early French marble-topped bombe commode makes the perfect surface for an English drinks table. Drinks on show include the King's Ginger, invented by Berry Bros. and Rudd to "warm and revivify" King Edward VII after long drives in his open-topped Daimler.

P. G. Wodehouse was a great chronicler of the country house cocktail and the importance of the drinks table. In *Laughing Gas*, he describes Reggie, the third Earl of Havershot, overcome with a sudden thirst for alcohol. "It seemed to me that if I didn't climb outside something moist in about half a jiffy, I should expire in dreadful agonies. And this thought had scarcely flitted into my mind when I noticed that all the materials for a modest binge were hospitably laid out on a table in the corner. There was the good old decanter, the jolly old syphon, the merry bucket of ice, and, in brief, the whole bag of tricks. They seemed to be beckoning to me, and I tottered across like a camel making for an oasis and started mixing."

But mixing what exactly? Wodehouse doesn't specify in this instance, but in other books he happily extols the virtues of various cocktails, not least for their morale-boosting properties that could make one feel that one "could bite a tiger" (as Gussie Fink-Nottle once famously exclaimed). He describes martinis and mint juleps but also absurdist creations like the May Queen. "Its foundation is any good, dry champagne, to which is added liqueur brandy, Armagnac, kummel, yellow chartreuse and old stout, to taste." An alarming concoction indeed.

In general, the English prefer traditional cocktails rather than the outré and over-engineered creations of contemporary mixologists. The art

expert and country house aficionado Alexander Hope favours the old-school classics. "A White Lady, Gin and It, or an original lime daiquiri—not one of the ridiculous modern versions." The daiquiri, with its basic recipe of rum, sugar, and lime juice, can trace its roots back to Royal Navy "grog"—a concoction doled out to sailors from the eighteenth century onwards to ward off scurvy and presumably stiffen the sinews for the fierce naval battles of the Napoleonic Wars. It's debatable whether Admiral Lord Nelson would have looked kindly on a frozen strawberry version.

The drinks table is important because it shows a generosity of spirit (or, if you'll forgive the pun, a generosity of spirits) and is the most obvious and immediate symbol of a host who desires nothing more than the comfort of his guests. For why dictate what or how much or when they should drink when you can leave them to their own blissful devices? There is also an element of discretion about it, as opposed to publicly asking what someone would like to drink. Teetotallers might sometimes feel embarrassed by sounding like killjoys, and serious imbibers might feel ashamed by asking for the enormous whiskey they truly desire.

> The drinks table is important because it shows a generosity of spirit (or, if you'll forgive the pun, a generosity of spirits) and is the most obvious and immediate symbol of a host who desires nothing more than the comfort of his guests.

To create a drinks table, you need to start with the table itself. The concept is actually a relatively modern one that came into fashion in the 1920s with the invention of the cocktail. Hence, there are no original antique tables specifically built to hold drinks, and all the drinks tables that you find in country houses today are repurposed. They might be old desks, or sideboards, gaming or card tables, marble-topped consoles, circular hall tables or even pianos. Alexander Hope's own one is an eighteenth-century writing table by Gillows of Lancaster with a thick piece of glass cut to size and overlaid on top. Next, the equipment: a cocktail shaker, obviously. In an ideal world, this would be an original silver one from the 1930s by a wonderful maker such as Asprey. Then crystal mixing glasses, strainers, long spoons, jiggers, muddlers, and so on. A chopping board, knife, and lemons, mint, and cucumber. A corkscrew with its handle fashioned out of an antler is a handsome thing, and a bottle opener. Some people use vintage scent bottles as atomisers for vermouth. And most importantly: ice. You can't make a good drink without it. It needs to be plentiful and regularly replenished. There are some fantastic silver and china ice buckets but, on our travels for this book, we spied several of the generously sized, insulated, rattan ones made by OKA. Mixers, which are sometimes cunningly hidden under a piece of tapestry below the table. And then, of course a good range of spirits. Gin is of primary importance (with Gilpin's being especially popular) but the English like as eclectic a selection as possible, and you will often find some

Opposite: A fine early nineteenth-century writing table by the famed cabinetmaker Gillows of Lancaster. The owner has had a thick piece of glass cut to size and overlaid on top to protect the mahogany and make it easy to wipe clean. Highballs, tumblers, and martini glasses are lined up on top, ready for action, alongside a generous array of spirits, including Matthew Gilpin's excellent gin.

extremely obscure tinctures. The famed interior decorator Emma Burns has a bottle of spirit distilled from mistletoe alongside her bottles of Campari, for instance.

The classic song book of country house cocktails includes the Negroni, the dry martini, and the Brandy Alexander (made famous by Anthony Blanche in *Brideshead Revisited*, who drank four on the trot, "down the little red lane they go"). But the White Lady reigns supreme. James and Laura Duckworth-Chad, of Castle Hill in Devon, are fans. "I suppose you might call it the house cocktail," says James. "My parents-in-law liked making them, and we served them at our wedding." And they are also prominent in country house literature, featuring in the novels of both Agatha Christie and Dorothy L. Sayers—whose protagonist, the amateur detective Lord Peter Wimsey, was keen on them.

But, of course, anything goes at the drinks table. The hospitable host aims to provide the widest spectrum of spirits, mixers, bitters, and other accoutrements in order to let his guests mix the exact drink that they feel like, unencumbered by the prejudices, tastes, or measurements of others—whether that be an elderflower cordial and soda or something a bit stronger. Because sometimes, even in the comfortable confines of the English country house, a stiff drink is called for.

Opposite: It comes as no surprise that Sam and Georgie Pearman have an exemplary drinks table, because both are consummate hosts who run some of the finest pubs in the country. In their home near Stroud, they use an old planning chest with a zinc top as the surface for their bottles.

Right: A drinks cabinet created out of an antique commode in the drawing room of Southrop Manor.

Opposite: The drinks table of interior decorator Emma Burns in her "book barn" library in Oxfordshire. Next to the table is a cantilevered door (covered with book-filled shelves) that leads through to a pantry with a fridge for mixers and wine.

Above left: The marble-topped drinks table in Phoebe Dickinson's hall came from Philip Adler Antiques in Tetbury. The lamp was found at auction.

Above right: A very prettily decorated drinks table in Salthrop House, home of Sophie Conran

Left: The walls in this drawing room are a glowing yellow, varnished by specialist painter David Mendel. At night, its slight shine reflects the firelight, giving the room a wonderful warmth. The chairs are covered in old Colefax and Fowler curtains sourced by Natalia Violet Antiques.

The watercolour painting above the drinks is *Waiting for an Audience with the Pacha* by Arthur Melville.

Above: In the sitting room of interior decorator Carlos Garcia's house in Norfolk. The drinks sit on an antique bamboo tray table dating to the nineteenth century. Above it hang two small oils on board of Suffolk landscapes by Kate Giles. The curtains are Robert Kime—based on a state bed at Hardwick Hall in Derbyshire. Carlos uses this table to mix Negronis in the summer and dirty martinis in the winter.

9

The Sofa

The sofa is the place for gossiping, romancing, game playing, and debating. Not to mention daydreaming, newspaper rustling, and napping.

Previous spread, left: A fabulous, formal antique settee against the wall in this kitchen in Norfolk. Claude, the wirehaired dachshund, sits under a portrait of an Elizabethan lady.

Previous spread, right: In James Mackie's "book room," he has put an early twentieth-century sofa covered in Bennison's Wabi Sabi against the main bookcase, which is topped with a classical pediment.

Above: A sofa in the sitting room end of a pretty bedroom in the Cotswolds decorated by Joanna Wood. The cushions are a mixture of antique and custom made that reflect the needlepoint Aubusson rug.

Six nights a week, for more than seventy years, a large audience has filed into St. Martin's Theatre in London to watch a performance of Agatha Christie's classic whodunnit *The Mousetrap*. They take their seats in the hushed and darkened auditorium, and when the curtain rises on the longest-running play in the world, they find themselves transported to the interior of a fictional Berkshire manor house named Monkswell. In the centre of the stage sits a large sofa (covered in a William Morris floral fabric called Compton). It is around this sofa that all the drama, intrigue, and action takes place, just as it does around the sofa in all English country houses.

The sofa originally evolved from the bench, explains Edward Bulmer (the architectural historian and interior decorator), as we visit his charming Queen Anne house in Herefordshire. The word is Turkish and is derived from the Arabic word *suffah*, meaning *ledge* or *bench*. Early sofas were hard and unforgiving, but from the early nineteenth century, people started to desire more comfortable furniture, and, as Bulmer puts it, sofas quickly became "lumps of upholstery with legs" (albeit supremely elegant lumps).

One of the early pioneers of this new style was the legendary furniture company Howard & Sons, founded in 1820. John Howard and his son

George used innovative techniques and designs to create armchairs and sofas so feted that they were commissioned by the owners of stately homes throughout the country and by Queen Victoria herself. The company still exists today and makes sofas that are considered by many to be the epitome of comfort. And antique versions of classic designs such as "Bridgewater" are incredibly sought after. Marcus Spencer, who specialises in the curation and restoration of antique sofas, describes how "high quality seating improves with age because the horsehair takes our body form and springs soften and the jute products relax, creating that unmistakable 'caught and held' feeling when you sit back and relax into 'a cloud of comfort.'"

A vibrant green sofa by George Smith covered in a Romo linen fabric stands out against the dark panelling in Edward Bulmer's sitting room in Herefordshire.

Opposite: A chaise longue with cushions designed by Jessica Fleming, covered in a Penny Morrison fabric. A Pooky lampshade on an antique lampstand. The antique bookcase was bought at a reclamation yard and fitted and painted into the panelling with Farrow & Ball Light Blue.

Left: A pared-back sitting room in Dorset. On the sofa is a Fine Cell Work cushion picturing a quail. These cushions are handmade by inmates of British prisons. Above the sofa is a picture of an eighteenth-century girl carrying a posy. And on the table behind the sofa is an eclectic collection of decorative items, including some Nepalese beads, a handmade model of a World War I tank, and a home-grown pumpkin.

Of course, there are hundreds of sofa types and dozens of companies in England that make them. But there are certain classical designs that are perennially popular in the country house. Scroll arms are often favoured, as are Chesterfields with their deep-buttoned upholstery (most commonly rendered in leather) and their rolled arms that continue at a similar height around the back. There is also the iconic Knowle sofa whose sides are tied to the back with heavy decorative braid attached to exposed wooden finials. Lots of styles are suitable but what they have in common is a commitment to the comfort of their inhabitants with deep seats and proper feather-filled cushions. They should always be welcoming, like an old friend. The Victorian novelist William Makepeace Thackeray (author of *Vanity Fair*) puts it best: "I want a sofa, as I want a friend, upon which I can repose familiarly. If you can't have intimate terms and freedom with one and the other, they are of no good."

It is in the drawing room where the sofa reigns supreme. This is a room that is inevitably more feminine than its opposite number, the dining room. Traditionally, this is where ladies would withdraw to after dinner in order to drink coffee or a tisane of some sort whilst the men stayed put at the table with their port and politics and cigars. It also was, and remains, the place to take afternoon tea, where the lady of the house would perch daintily on the edge of the sofa and pour Earl Grey into bone china cups for her guests. This outmoded role-playing and separation of the sexes is now (largely) consigned to the past, but the inherent femininity of the drawing room remains in most country houses. So, these rooms are often painted in delicate colours and filled with flowers and masses of soft cushions and pretty objets d'art. And the sofas themselves are often covered in pale linens or floral fabrics—most traditionally, chintz. This, originally, was a woodblock-printed, plain-weave cotton fabric from India with a polished finish and bold designs featuring flowers and other patterns. But in its modern sense, it means any bright floral pattern on a light background. Chintz fell out of fashion, partly due to overuse in the latter half of the twentieth century, but is now as popular as ever in the English country house because of its traditional look and unabashed, cheerful beauty.

Of course, the sofa isn't only to be found in the drawing room. You may find sofas in sitting rooms, in the corners of kitchens, at the ends of beds, and even in bathrooms. Edward Bulmer advises that, if there is the space, one should always leave an old sofa in the corner of a room "as a comfortable outpost" and describes them as being "as much a part of the country house look as dogs or books."

In fact, if you were to attempt to describe the entire English country house aesthetic in a single phrase, it might be *elegant comfort*, and if you were to point to a single object that encapsulates this, it is the sofa.

Opposite: The sofa in this sitting room was originally a Knowle (you can still see the knobs), but the owner cut the tall arms off. It is covered with a "very old" quilt found in a French market. The main picture above (of a table) is by the famed figurative painter Emily Patrick.

The china owls are contemporary. The owner had them converted into lamps and fitted with ikat shades. On the floor to the right of the sofa is a sculpture of a much-loved pug by Nicola Toms. ("I adore it," says the owner, "although my husband asks why anyone would want to look at a dog's fanny.")

Left: The drawing room at the Court of Noke in Herefordshire, or, as its owner Edward Bulmer calls it, "the music room." A butter-soft pink leather sofa reflects the pink of curtains made from Anokhi tablecloths. The room is painted in Pomona, a color from Bulmer's own collection of natural paints.

Above: An oil painting of a sofa by Phoebe Dickinson, hanging in her studio in Gloucestershire

Above: A classic Knowle sofa from Lorfords, which its owner, Jessica Fleming, covered in some "deeply inexpensive velvet whose red seemed a bit bright when it first arrived so we employed the dogs to beat it up a bit."

Right: A Knowle-style sofa but without the ties at Warmwell House in Dorset. Above the sofa is a portrait of Miss Crawley (an ancestor of the present owner) painted in the 1600s by Francis Cotes (one of the founding members of the Royal Academy alongside the likes of Joshua Reynolds and Thomas Gainsborough).

The magnificent saloon of Castle
Hill in Devon

Opposite, left: A drawing room in Norfolk decorated by Birdie Fortescue. A Jamb sofa is covered in a Colefax and Fowler chenille, with a mixture of cushions covered in Safi suzani material and pink silk from Claremont. The walls are covered in Phillip Jeffries green raffia, which creates a calming backdrop for the eclectic collection of paintings.

Opposite, below left: Birdie Fortescue's own sitting room. The sofa is English, late nineteenth century, and covered in an off-white chevron. The cushions are a "mishmash" of past designs of Birdie's.

A soft red-painted raffia lampshade. Behind the sofa is a Patrice Mesnier horse sculpture. And behind that a French eighteenth-century bookcase with a scrolled Italian giltwood decorative pediment above.

Opposite, below right: A sofa covered with a Colefax and Fowler floral on linen with a bullion fringe. The green paint on the walls is by Edward Bulmer.

Right: A traditional Knowle sofa, with its huge, flap-down side-arms, makes a perfect spot for reading. This one is covered in a Charlotte fabric from India.

10

The Desk

When people bemoan the lost art of letter writing,
they might be pleased to know that the tradition
remains alive in the English country house.

Previous spread, left: An unusual desk in the staircase hall of Castle Hill. It has large open sides for storing huge folios, albums, and ledgers. On top of the desk is where the family keep their visitors' books—one for people and one for dogs!

Previous spread, right: A fine William and Mary bureau desk in Caryn Hibbert's bedroom at Southrop manor, from where she writes her thank-you letters. The chair is covered in a Fermoie fabric.

Above: An artist's studio in Gloucestershire looking out over a garden full of sculpture. The desk and surrounding cabinetry are painted in Tropical Palm by Sanderson.

Opposite: A George III mahogany Carlton House writing table in the drawing room at Buscot Park in Oxfordshire—home of Lord Faringdon. A French Empire gilt bronze ormolu mantel clock sits on the desk. The shield-back chair in front is late eighteenth century by Seddon, Sons and Shackleton.

The English love a letter. They like writing them, they certainly like receiving them, and their libraries are full of volumes celebrating the letter-writing skills of others (Evelyn Waugh and Nancy Mitford's correspondence with one another being a classic example).

Letters are far more meaningful than their unlovely relation the email. They are physically beautiful, tactile, and treasured. No one ties a ribbon around a bundle of emails and keeps them in a desk drawer for future generations to discover. The inspiration behind letters is often gratitude, commiseration, or love, and writing them takes time and consideration. Reading them takes time as well, particularly nowadays when we are out of the habit of deciphering handwriting.

The trend away from putting fountain pen to paper and towards working exclusively on a laptop has reduced the importance of the desk. It's easy to tap away at your emails in bed, or perch at a kitchen counter, or sit in an

armchair in Starbucks with your computer literally in your lap. But none of these places allow you to sit up straight with a high, flat surface in front of you and write elegantly.

Desks have a romance and history to them. Other pieces of furniture are just sat on or used for storing clothes. But when you sit at an antique desk, you are aware that others, perhaps forebears, perhaps strangers, have sat here before. What were they writing or thinking about? Were they pouring their hearts out into love letters, or writing speeches of political importance? Can you hear the echo of shuffled papers and scratchy fountain pens and the whispers of those mouthing as they write? Stroking the leather top of an old desk gives you a tangible sense of the past.

> Desks have a romance and history to them. Other pieces of furniture are just sat on or used for storing clothes. But when you sit at an antique desk, you are aware that others, perhaps forebears, perhaps strangers, have sat here before.

There is a myriad of types: secretaires, roll tops, leather-topped pedestal desks, drawered writing tables (like the supremely elegant George III Carlton House desk in the drawing room at Buscot Park), campaign desks, davenports, kneeholes, drop-fronted bureaus—the list is endless. They can be found in studies, morning rooms, corners of kitchens, and, crucially, bedrooms. Bedroom desks have a long tradition. Writing anything, be it diary, letter, or novel requires peace and quiet, and the bedchamber offers a place of sanctuary, away from the noise and bustle of the rest of the house. In times past, ladies would habitually attend to their correspondence in their bedroom. Their maid would bring them tea and the morning's post, and they would read their letters in bed before getting up and dashing off replies from a secretaire in the corner of the room.

Times may have moved on, but bedroom desks remain relevant. Children's bedrooms need them so homework can be done and intricate Airfix models made (and violent video games played). And a good hostess will always place them in guest bedrooms, with the gracious assumption that her visitors would like to keep up with their own written correspondence (or, more likely, be able to join a work Zoom call in privacy).

Sometimes dressing tables are used to double up as desks, but most often, bedrooms contain purpose-built bureau bookcases. A bureau, also known as a *secretaire*, also known as an *escritoire*, also known as a *dropleaf desk*, also known as a *writing cabinet* (do keep up), is a desk that takes the form of a chest of drawers topped by a hinged flap that opens to reveal a writing surface. This, in turn, is often topped by a bookcase. It is a substantial piece of furniture and extremely useful because of its multifaceted nature, its storage capabilities, and its clean lines when closed. The desk area generally has a series of pigeonholes and small drawers for hiding treasures that have

Opposite: A small antique pedestal desk in a child's bedroom, for homework and essential model building

Above: Sophie Conran's desk at Salthrop. It is a cherrywood French library table gifted to her by her parents on the occasion of her twenty-first birthday.

Opposite: A Victorian partners desk in the window of a library in Somerset. Bouquets of flowers sit under the pair of glass domes. The ones on the left are fashioned out of shells. The ones on the right are knitted. The man on the horse is a maquette of Marshal Joffre by George Malissard.

to be closed before the writing surface is secured. Secretaires have a bonus of being easily lockable, thereby keeping trinkets of affection and salacious love letters safe. Romantic heroines keep the key on a chain around their necks.

An age-old aphorism suggests that a cluttered desk is a sign of a cluttered mind. But you would expect nothing less in a maximalist English country house. The typical English desk, if not untidy, certainly has quite a lot on it. Classic accoutrements, of sometimes questionable use, abound: blotters, inkwells, calendars, and letter racks. And then there are books, photographs, flowers, small busts, and little ornaments of every description imaginable. Plus, almost as a matter of course, diaries, notebooks, and writing paper, all made by Smythson. In their fight against the digital takeover of life, the English like to spend soothingly large amounts of money at the New Bond Street headquarters of this smartest of stationers.

I have a great friend who, to this day, closes the envelope of every letter she writes with a wax seal. She sits at her desk with her wax beads, candle warmer, and melting spoon. Instead of a signet ring, she uses a stamp with a wooden grip to press her monogrammed seal (which is her initial surrounded by a Napoleonic wreath) into the molten wax. She admits that it is just a bit of silliness, but when one falls heavily through my letter box amidst a flurry of junk mail and utilities bills, I am utterly delighted. Long live the letter!

Right: The burr walnut bureau in Carlos Garcia's bedroom is a nineteenth-century reproduction of an original eighteenth-century piece. The cane-and-bamboo chair is Victorian. The flowers (from Carlos's cutting garden) are held in a clever Sibyl Colefax and John Fowler vase. The lamp base is an old alabaster vase that Carlos converted with an antique fabric shade from Robert Kime. The painting (bought at auction) is by Phillipa Maynard Romer.

Opposite: Edward Bulmer's desk in his drawing room in Herefordshire. The walls are painted in Pomona—one of Bulmer's range of natural paints.

Opposite: A bureau in the sitting room at Warmwell House. A decorative silver woodcock sits next to the clock on the top. Above hangs a *Vanity Fair* Spy cartoon of Lt. Colonel Archie Crawley of the Grenadier Guards—a forebear of the present owner.

Right: A George II bureau bookcase in two parts, made from finely figured flame mahogany.

The blue china on the top of furniture like this has been a popular decorative trope since the eighteenth century.

Left: The bust above this writing desk at Castle Hill is of Susan, Viscountess Ebrington (the courtesy title of the Earls Fortescue), who died aged thirty-one in 1827.

Opposite: A writing desk in the saloon of Castle Hill, home to James and Laura Duckworth-Chad. The desk is adorned, in a typical fashion, with family photographs.

Opposite: A French Louis XVI mahogany kneehole desk with a leather top, which once belonged to the South African mining magnate Sir Lionel Phillips. On the desk is a bust of Samuel Whitbread (of the brewing family) by George Garrard.

Right: Jessica Fleming's desk in the house designed by her architect husband, Christian. The leather-topped writing table comes from Christian's father, the author James Fleming (himself the nephew of spy writer Ian Fleming). The backless tub chair is covered in a very pale, faded green velvet. Christian designed this bay window specifically to house a desk so Jessica could sit here and enjoy the fabulous views in both directions of the valley below.

11

The Four-Poster Bed

Non-afficionados are puzzled as to the point of a four-poster bed, but they are considered essential to the English country house, and you will often find them crammed into tiny cottage guest bedrooms as well as in the state bedrooms of the stateliest of homes.

As a child I was captivated by the story "The Princess and the Pea." This Hans Christian Andersen fairy tale describes a prince struggling to find a suitably high-born bride to marry. One stormy night, a young woman appears at his castle door seeking shelter. She claims to be a princess, but the prince's mother has her doubts. So, the queen decides to test their unexpected guest by offering her a four-poster bed to sleep in. On the bed she has her servants pile up twenty mattresses, and under the mattresses she places a single pea. In the morning, the girl, when questioned, tells of having had a sleepless night because of something hard in the bed. The queen then realises she must be of royal birth after all, as no one but a real princess could be so delicate. Leaving the rank snobbery and social engineering aside, what was so beguiling about this tale was the thought of the giant four-poster bed with its feather-soft mattresses being a refuge from the howling winds and thrashing rain outside.

I am not alone in being captured by the magic and romance of the four-poster. But what is it that makes them a country house staple, and why has their appeal endured down through the centuries? It is because of their multifaceted nature. They are both opulently beautiful and practical at the same time.

The four-poster originated in the Middle Ages. They were a way to ensure privacy in an era when one's servants might sleep on mats next to the bed. Even more importantly, their curtains provided warmth in poorly

heated houses. And in medieval times, before eaves were closed and windows glazed, the canopies would protect the occupants from bird droppings. In modern times, their protection is more symbolic, but there is no doubting the sense of peace and security they provide.

They also have a certain undeniable sex appeal about them. They create an immediate intimate space that engenders amorous feelings. What's more, the sturdy posts and roped tiebacks are a fantastic setting for all manner of naughty fantasy and role play. The occupants might stare up at the canopy and imagine the billowing sails of a pirate ship or the rippling folds of a Bedouin tent. But more than this, the four-poster bed provides an opportunity for the English to indulge in their greatest passion of all: fabric.

> The occupants might stare up at the canopy and imagine the billowing sails of a pirate ship or the rippling folds of a Bedouin tent. But more than this, the four-poster bed provides an opportunity for the English to indulge in their greatest passion of all: fabric.

The English love fabric of all type, texture, pattern, and hue, and their bedrooms are adorned with silk curtains, velvet-covered chaises longues, chintzes, linen sheets, cashmere blankets, and more. This is where the four-poster bed comes into play. It provides a further canvas for lavishly upholstering, draping, brocading, and tasselling. Traditionally, a four-poster would have a solid oak frame supporting a ceiling known as a *tester*. Outer and inner valances or pelmets would hide the iron rails and rings from which the curtains could be hung and drawn across to prevent drafts entering. Nowadays of course, with central heating and an absence of servants dossing down on the floor next to one, these curtains rarely need to be drawn and more often than not are fixed in place for purely decorative purposes.

The interior decorator Carlos Garcia is a huge fan. "Four-poster beds are an indulgence, but they are so comforting, like a cocoon." In his own bedroom in his Norfolk farmhouse, he has an original George III mahogany bed by the famous eighteenth-century cabinetmaker Gillows of Lancaster. It is covered in a pretty floral pattern with a plain cream interior. The fabric of the canopy is gathered into a traditional sunburst ceiling, "as I wanted something purposefully old-fashioned." Carlos also has a four-poster in his main guest bedroom. This one is covered in a bold fabric of his own making. It is based on an antique Ottoman headscarf with a Kandili handblock print that Carlos found on a recent trip to Istanbul. He brought it home and copied the design to create his own linen. Furthering the theme, Carlos commissioned a local artisan to hand-tie over three thousand tassels, which he has used to trim the curtains and pelmet. As he explains, "These are the sort of decorations one might have seen in a traditional central Asian yurt."

The designer Sophie Conran is also a great advocate of the four-poster. Nearly all of the bedrooms in Salthrop house (her exquisite eighteenth-

Left: Carlos Garcia's guest bedroom (for both humans and dogs) is decorated with a fabric created by Carlos himself. It is based on an original nineteenth-century Turkish Kandili that Carlos found in Istanbul.

century manor house on the edge of the Marlborough Downs) have one. Bucking the trend for the purely decorative, her own bed has proper working rails and curtains, which she pulls across every night. She adores the cosy enclave this creates, and it also allows her to forgo curtains and leave the beautiful Georgian sash windows of her bedroom unadorned.

Four-poster bedrooms are often quite feminine in nature and are decorated with the lady of the house in mind. Her husband would normally have his own dressing room next door, filled with his suits and shoes and brushes. This room might also contain an austere single bed where the husband can be banished for snoring or other boorish behaviour. Ideally, the four-poster will sit on the back wall of the bedroom opposite the windows. Underneath, or between the windows, should be a dressing table and looking glass. A pair of bedside tables with plenty of room for housing books, as well as a water jug and flowers, are a must. Not to mention a pair of lamps whose shades give a further avenue for fabric indulgence.

Other furniture in the room might include a sofa or chaise longue. These allow the bedroom to double up as a private sitting room or boudoir—which comes from the French word *bouder*, meaning "to pout or sulk." That makes this the perfect place to huffily escape to avoid one's annoying family or guests. And with this usage, once again, the four-poster bedroom is a refuge that no country house can do without.

Above: Sophie Conran's four-poster bed with working rails that let her pull the curtains across at night

Opposite: Every bedroom needs a place to recline and read a book (or somewhere to toss clothes). This chaise longue with a view over the garden is ideal.

Left: A guest bedroom at Bellamont. Both walls and curtains are covered in a Nina Campbell print—Barbary Toile.

Above: A domed four-poster guest bedroom in the house belonging to interior decorator Amanda Hornby. The bed is dressed in a Bennison fabric with a Jean Monro lining and has unusual painted candy-striped pillars.

Opposite: A guest bedroom at the Court of Noke, the home of architectural historian and paint maker Edward Bulmer

Above: This rococo-style four-poster bed in Buscot Park is completely dressed in a heavy cotton calico.

Above: Looking across her four-poster to the dressing table in Harriet Sykes's bedroom at Bellamont. You can see the sunburst canopy of the bed in the looking glass. Mirrored-frame floral prints add to this bedroom's prettiness.

Left: This, obviously, is not a four-poster, but it does have a charming crown canopy and the most deliciously squidgy pink sofa at its foot—English country house charm personified.

Opposite: A bedroom in the Cotswolds decorated by legendary interior decorator Joanna Wood. The contemporary carved four-poster is by Beaudesert in a Heppelwhite style. The bedside tables are George II mahogany tray–topped commodes with sang-de-boeuf pots converted into lamps.

The master bedroom of an eighteenth-century manor house in Gloucestershire. The red chinoiserie mirror adds a fabulous splash of vibrant colour.

12

The Bath

Whereas modern shower rooms are temples of hygiene and convenience, country house bathrooms are pleasure domes dedicated to relaxation and rejuvenation. The English are fetishistic about baths, and the sometimes-questionable pleasures of country sports and activities are only made bearable by the thought of a good soak afterwards.

It was the ancient Romans who first introduced baths to the English—and they were taken to with relish. What started as public facilities transformed, over the centuries, into singular baths in private houses, and the bathtub today is a much-cherished icon in the English country house.

Sir Winston Churchill—history's greatest Englishman—was a serious devotee. He would take two lengthy hot baths every day, even during the peak of the Second World War. There he would scrub himself furiously with Brown Windsor soap—a strong-smelling concoction of lavender, bergamot, cassia, and clove that was also a favourite of Queen Victoria. He would also sometimes work from the bath and shout dictation to his long-suffering secretaries who would sit on the other side of the bathroom door listening to his barkings as he splashed about. (Indeed, senior military commanders would sometimes attend to him whilst in the bathroom. And once, famously, when staying at the White House in 1941, President Franklin D. Roosevelt

called on Churchill in the guest quarters to find him having just risen from the bath and striding around the room naked "all pink and white" shouting orders to his staff. Roosevelt made his apologies, but Churchill brushed them away saying, "You see, Mr. President, I have nothing to hide from you.")

The bathroom should be a sanctuary and an oasis of calm. Physically, the bath is a place for easing the muscles, exfoliating the skin, and stimulating the nervous system. But it is also a place for reading, contemplation, plotting, and beautifying oneself for the evening ahead.

Of course, the most important feature of the country house bathroom is the bath itself. Classically this should be a free-standing roll-top, made of enamelled cast iron, and, more often than not, with ball-and-claw feet in the style of Victorian bathtubs. These claw-foot terminals are said to derive from an ancient Chinese motif of a dragon clutching a precious stone in its talon, representing the preservation of purity—an ideal theme for the Victorian bathroom whose moralists firmly believed in the Christian aphorism that "cleanliness is next to godliness."

Generally, the bath should be placed away from the wall in a prominent place in keeping with its stature as the raison d'être of the room. And, ideally, near to a long window with a beautiful view. This central placement also helps avoid water from splashing onto paintwork or delicate wallpapers. For an English country house bathroom is not a marble shrine whose glossy, polished surfaces can be easily wiped and dried. Instead, the bathroom is a warm and cosy enclave full of soft natural materials.

Flooring is important. No one wants a cold, slippery floor. Something softer is required. A fitted carpet divides opinion: Some people love the look and feel, others find it (literally) a step too far to rise from a bath and place a sopping wet foot onto absorbent deep-pile carpet. It's almost too decadent. A compromise is to use rush matting or sisal. Not as comfortable underfoot, but it gives a warm, organic feel to the room. Or lay rugs (antique or modern) onto wooden floorboards.

In cold houses, a working fireplace is the ultimate dream. Could anything be more heavenly than to bathe while listening to the crackle of burning wood in a room lit by flickering flames, and then afterwards to stand in front of the fire holding open your bath towel like a vampire's cloak to dry your body? But a non-working fireplace (or one that you are too lazy or mean to light) is still a lovely architectural detail, with its mantel shelf maybe decorated with shells and other less formal objets than you might find above a drawing room fireplace.

The English country house bathroom should be lovely and inviting and decorated to delight. In fact, once the basic plumbing and fixtures are in place, one should ignore the functionality of the

The English country house bathroom should be lovely and inviting and decorated to delight.

Above: Attic bathrooms don't have to be plain and should be decorated with as much thought as all others. The set of images above this bath are paintings on old treasury bonds found in the Maharajah's craft market in Jaipur.

Opposite: Clemmie Fraser's wonderful bathroom at Waverton just gets better. A floral-print armchair, a bespoke dressing table and mirror, a generously sized tray table for books and bath salts, and a picture wall full of delights

room and decorate it much like any other. Importantly, for example, there should be art on the walls. This will often have a botanical theme, as the English are always trying to bring surrounding nature into a room. Antique floral prints are popular, often hung as a group. Or how about a mural or trompe l'oeil like in Sophie Crossley's bathroom in her Norfolk manor house? Here she commissioned the artist Paola Cumiskey to cover the whole room in a depiction of the surrounding parkland. The work incorporates Sophie's children's favourite animals from the garden and park beyond. Real flowers are popular as well. And I am particularly taken by the Somerset bathroom (featured on page 190) whose owner has joyfully let a creeping wisteria on the outside of the house enter through the sash window to hang decorously over the bath.

A comfortable armchair is essential—for collapsing into when you have risen too quickly from an overly hot bath or for a spouse or friend to sit on and chat to you whilst you soak. My grandmother used to have a wonderful squishy one that was covered in a towelling material.

And, last but not least, a bookshelf. For there is no more superlative pleasure than reading something transporting whilst using one's big toe to fiddle with the tap and keep the hot water topped up.

Left: A fabulous picture
wall in Sophie Conran's
luminescent pink bathroom
in Wiltshire

Above: A detail of the pink
bathroom. The oval antique
gilt mirror and scallop-
edged candy-striped
wastepaper bin are pretty
touches.

Above: Jessica Fleming's own bathroom in the Cotswolds. The yellow tub is from the Cast Iron Bath Company and is painted Sudbury Yellow by Farrow & Ball. The chaise longue is from Lorfords Antiques. "I sit on the chaise longue, Christian lies in the bath, and we catch up on the day."

Left: Steve Price, a Norfolk-based cabinetmaker, made this bath surround at Beck Hall. The Maltese cross replicates the crosses on the "very antique" Maltese chest of drawers, a nod to where the owner's father was based with the army.

Opposite: This bathroom in paint maker Edward Bulmer's Herefordshire home is painted in Olympian Green—a lime green with great warmth.

A fabulous bath (from Drummonds) in the curved triple bay window of this bedroom in Oxfordshire. A vintage hatbox sits on top of the antique linen press.

Opposite: A bathroom decorated by Jessica Fleming, who loves to convert antique furniture (sideboards, commodes, chests of drawers) into sinks. She buys them from antiques shops and then has marble tops cut and gets them plumbed in. She likes her bathrooms to have wooden floors with rugs on top.

Right: A bathroom belonging to Birdie Fortescue, painted Ball Green from Farrow & Ball and with a Vanderhurd rug

13

The Dog

Possibly the most important decorative motif in the
English country house is The Dog. Whether living
or represented in art, you will find the canine form
everywhere.

Previous spread, left: Noble, heraldic Talbot dogs as finials on the gateposts at Bellamont. The Talbot was a white hunting hound common in England during the Middle Ages.

Previous spread, right: Christian Fleming designed the giant island in his kitchen around this triple bay alcove for his dogs, Pooch, Buddy, and Queenie. "Dogs always want to be at the centre of the action, so this allows them to be at the heart of family life but simultaneously slightly out of the way."

Above: The dogs visitors' book at Castle Hill

Opposite: Lottie the spaniel and Honey the golden retriever at home in the boot room of their Georgian country house in Oxfordshire. With their Sophie Allport beds, a wood-burning stove, and a massive basket of balls and assorted dog toys, life is pretty good.

I n the entrance hall of every country house in England, you will invariably find a leather-bound visitors book. Neo-Palladian Castle Hill in North Devon is no exception. However, the book there, which sits proudly on a desk at the bottom of the grand staircase, is intended purely for visitors of a canine nature. Recorded in it are all the dogs that have stayed in the house over the last century or so. The dogs are recorded by their first name and the family name of their owners, along with comments detailing their exploits during their visit. These include: "Chased some visitors and enjoyed lying on the sofa," and "Attacked her hostess. Possible turd on stairs?" It is a book that perfectly encapsulates the English attitude towards their dogs and reminds us that no country house is complete without (at least) one.

We started the chapter on boot rooms by naming it as the place where the dog lives. This is not strictly true. The boot room may be the official residence of the dog. This is where it has a bed, is where it is dried off and fed, where it is sent when in disgrace. But the fact is, dogs like to be wherever the action is, and their owners like them by their side. So, in reality, a dog has several resting places: a daybed in the hall, a cushion in front of the Aga, a rug on the sitting room sofa, a favourite armchair in the drawing room, a folded blanket on a chaise longue in a bedroom, and (close your ears if you are of a sensitive nature) occasionally their owner's bed itself. I know

several country-house dwellers who find it impossible to imagine sleeping without not just one but several dogs on their four-poster bed, and one countryman who claims to find it impossible to perform his conjugal duties correctly without the reassuring thump of a tail from his faithful Labrador in the corner of the bedroom.

Some dog beds are extremely luxurious—fully upholstered, bespokely made, and covered in tweed or, as in my husband's case, his clan's tartan. Wicker beds are popular. OKA, the home furnishings company set up by Viscountess Astor, sells extremely smart rattan creations that cost many hundreds of pounds. It is increasingly common to find special alcoves built into kitchen dressers or islands. Christian Fleming, who is one of England's leading contemporary architects of country houses, has built a triple bay range of berths under the giant island in his own kitchen to house his fox-red Labrador, Jackapoo, and toy Labradoodle. But the ultimate luxury, as far as most dogs are concerned, is a cushion in front of the Aga—the warmest place in the house, and one where the chance of a splash of stew landing on one's nose is a not-impossible dream.

Should one let one's dog on the sofa is a perennial country house debate and often leads to an absurd and byzantine set of rules whereby certain dogs are allowed on certain sofas on certain occasions or times of day. But it comes with the risk that a well-built and short-sighted

Above: A pair of dachshunds on a Lutyens bench underneath a dachshund-shaped planter

Opposite: Gimli's official bed in the boot room at Came House, surrounded by classic boot room paraphernalia, including a stuffed toy salmon, fishing nets, and a Coldstream Guards bearskin in its tin box

Should one let one's dog on the sofa is a perennial country house debate and often leads to an absurd and byzantine set of rules whereby certain dogs are allowed on certain sofas on certain occasions or times of day.

guest might mistake the family Pekingese for a fluffy cushion and sit on it. Stories abound in country house lore of just such happenings and unfortunate dogs being crushed or suffocated to death.

Before one picks the ideal bed, one has to pick the ideal dog. Some breeds are unquestionably more acceptable than others. The black Labrador is the quintessential country house dog. They are beautiful to behold, sleek-coated, loyal, and have an unparalleled lust for life. They are also exceptionally greedy. Spaniels are next in line, with working cockers the most favoured and Cavalier King Charles the least fashionable despite their ancient royal approval. Both Labradors and spaniels are not only faithful companions but also have an important use as gundogs. Some people separate these working dogs into outdoor kennels whilst allowing less useful but more pampered breeds the run of the house. The late, great Anthony Sykes used to let his "officer class" dogs in the house whilst his sheepdogs, which he termed *other ranks*, were housed outside.

Dachshunds are particularly popular. It was Queen Victoria who first brought them to prominence, but they temporarily fell out of favour during the Great War because of their German connection, when apparently people used to kick them in the street! The terrier class are particularly well liked, whether they be Norfolks, West Highland Whites, Patterdales, or Jack Russells. Elegant, slim breeds like whippets and lurchers seem particularly at home in the country house drawing room. And if you live in a very large house, then a Great Dane or Irish wolfhound fills the space nicely.

Then there are "amusing" dogs. Pointless small things who are loved for their ridiculousness; preposterous Pekingese, pugs with their absurdly curled tails and extraordinary snorting sounds, and crazed corgis (forever associated with Her Late Majesty Queen Elizabeth II). Their owners describe them with mock exasperation ("ludicrous animal!") but they are doted on as much as any child.

But although there might be a hierarchy of breeds when it comes to popularity and perceived poshness, the simple fact is that the English love all dogs—and with a stress on the plural.

But although there might be a hierarchy of breeds when it comes to popularity and perceived poshness, the simple fact is that the English love all dogs—and with a stress on the plural. It is perfectly normal to have three or more hounds, starting with a brace of Labradors or a trio of spaniels, then maybe a dachshund or two, and then a rescue mutt (possibly given to a youngest child as a companion).

Along with living beasts, the English country house is also a shrine to dogs past. Charcoal drawings of favourite pets hang in the boot room, whilst fine nineteenth-century oil paintings of faithful hounds hang in the drawing room along with bronze models. Country house art in general is often a celebration of all things canine.

Gimli, a fox-red Labrador, on the kitchen sofa at Came House. Gimli is named "after the ginger dwarf in *Lord of the Rings*," says Rags, her owner. Rags's children came up with the name after World Book Day, when they went to school dressed as characters from the Tolkien books.

Although dogs reign supreme, the English love of animals extends well beyond just them. "All creatures great and small, the English love them all" is how the popular hymn might be re-worded. A cat curled up on a window seat bathing in the sunlight is a familiar country house sight. Hamsters, guinea pigs, and chinchillas are to be found wherever there are children. Tortoises are not uncommon, although sadly, during our travels for this book, we never came across one decorated with diamonds like the one gifted to Julia in Evelyn Waugh's *Brideshead Revisited*. Chickens are often literally free-range to the extent that you might find them wandering about in a country house kitchen. And children (of all ages) are often found trying to smuggle all manner of other animals into the house, be they pigs, ponies, or peacocks. As always, the English love a house to be full of life and are unfussy about chaos or mess. One peer, whilst showing us around his library for this book, spotted a fossilised dog turd next to the fireplace. "I can't believe that's still here," he observed, before moving on, unbothered by its presence.

Opposite: Nutley and Ella in front of the fire in Sophie Conran's drawing room. The pair of pouffes (covered in a burgundy chenille) were a present from Sophie's brother, the designer Jasper Conran.

Above left: A portrait in pastels of the late, great Rory Bear the Labrador by Mouse Lesser (dogsbymouse.co.uk)

Above right: A doggy cushion on a chair used at the coronation of Her Late Majesty Queen Elizabeth II in 1953

Minka the whippet on her
bed under a writing table
in the drawing room at
Bellamont

This working cocker spaniel has its very own niche in this dresser made to fit the room by Suffolk cabinetmaker Pip Whittle. The owner painted it silver and has displayed a collection of Wemyss ware on its shelves.

Above: A bright pink sofa makes the ideal dog bed in the stair hall of Sophie Conran's house in Wiltshire. The ghostly figure on the stairs is Sophie's daughter, the fashion designer Coco Conran.

Right: Mouse, Sophie Conran's sweet-natured lurcher, has a special bed in the entrance hall of Salthrop House—an elegant sofa found in an antiques shop in Petworth. Mouse, who "has a bit of deerhound in her," needed a bed with a bit of scale.

Opposite: Dilys the lurcher in her official residence at Waverton House. The portrait on the wall is of her kennel mate Stanley the dachshund. The magnificent wallpaper is by Pierre Frey.

Left: Queenie the Labrador (born the day Queen Elizabeth II died) stretching out on a sofa made by Chloe Vestey, covered in a Pierre Frey weave. Dog rugs, to protect fine fabrics such as this, are an essential as the English are, on the whole, far too soft-hearted to ban dogs from sofas.

Above: Angelica (aka Jellybean) taking up residence in the corner of a George Smith sofa covered in a silk velvet (!) and a fabric from Bennison

Pudding, a cockapoo,
posing under her
portrait in Caroline
Baker's dining room in
the Cotswolds

Above left: A very doggy scene at Clemmie Fraser's house in Gloucestershire. Basil, the basset hound, sits in the hall next to a ceramic model of another basset. The china on the side table comes from Les Couilles de Chien on Golborne Road in London (literal translation: "the dog's bollocks").

Above right: Buddy the cockerpoo (aka Fat Lucy), at home on a Gainsborough armchair with claw-and-ball feet covered in a Guy Goodfellow flame stitch

14

Fun and Games

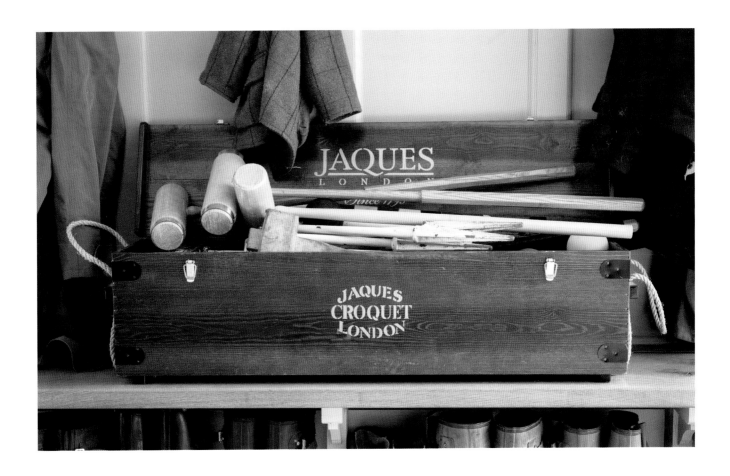

Despite its occasional grandeur, the English country
house doesn't take itself too seriously.

Page 220: Jessica Fleming larking about on her favourite hunter in her kitchen in Gloucestershire

Page 221: A classic Jaques croquet set in a boot room in Norfolk

Previous spread: Pig croquet on the front lawn at Castle Hill

Above: As if being stuffed weren't humiliation enough, taxidermy is frequently the brunt of various jokes. This hare was caught by the Quarme Harriers in 1926 and currently sports a pair of rose-tinted "Big Lips" sunglasses.

Opposite: Backgammon at Bellamont, overseen by a ceramic cat with a floating head

As I hope these pages have demonstrated, the owners of English country houses are keen for their homes not to be stuffy or overly formal environments. One of the key tenets of all interior decorators who champion the English country house look is that each room should have something silly or incongruous or, as Nancy Lancaster would put it, "something a little bit ugly" to prick its pomposity. And the English pride themselves on their sense of humour. So, when you walk around a country house, no matter how grand, you might find sunglasses on a statue, a paper hat stuck to an ancient portrait, amusing slogans embroidered onto cushions, framed political cartoons, comedically posed taxidermy, humorous Latin tags inscribed above a library bookcase, and so on. The English love the incongruous, the absurd, and the frivolous. Toward the end of her life, Nancy herself had an embroidered cushion in her bedroom inscribed with the words *Money is the root of all evil and women must have roots.* And even Her Late Majesty Queen Elizabeth II had a bright red cushion on a sofa in her drawing room at Balmoral emblazoned with the slogan *It's good to be Queen.*

Sometimes the humour is on a grand scale. Anthony Sykes had the motto *Coute que coute* engraved in huge letters on the front of his neo-Georgian house in Dorset. It's a pun in old French which could be loosely

translated as "Bugger the cost!" In the stick basket in Sophie Conran's house in Wiltshire, poking up through the umbrellas is a giant firework. It is a rocket containing her late father Sir Terence Conran's ashes, and on the front is written a quote from the great man himself: *If I can't smoke cigars in heaven, I shall not go.*

When the English aren't cracking jokes, they are playing games. Table tennis tables are often set up in entrance halls (the only room in the house big enough to accommodate them) and only packed away on the smartest of occasions. Billiards tables are also popular but they, however, require a permanent home and only large country houses can afford the space for the purpose-built rooms so beloved of the Victorians. Houses that do have billiards rooms find they are used more for Freda than anything else—a riotous after-dinner game involving large numbers of invariably drunk people hurling themselves around the table.

The English also love to play board games. When laziness or bad weather sets in, the library fire is stoked and the games cupboard is opened. Inside are battered old sets of *Monopoly*, *Cluedo*, *Scrabble*, and *Risk*. Backgammon sets are rife, as are purpose-built backgammon tables, often antique ones from France that were originally intended for Trictrac. And you can generally find a chess board or, even better, an already set-up game on an intricately inlaid wooden checkerboard table. Of course, what the English love playing most is cards: hearts, gin rummy, cheat, and shithead are all classics. Racing demon is chaotic fun when played on a giant ottoman in the drawing room, cleared of books. But the queen of all card games is bridge. Keen bridge players with large drawing rooms might have a permanently set-up card table with four chairs around it, ready for action. Failing that, a folding table with a green or red baize top is brought out after dinner. When there aren't enough keen players around to make up a four, these card tables double up as surfaces for puzzles, which often take weeks to be completed.

Some games take place outdoors. Every June, the world-famous Wimbledon Championships is hosted by the All England Club. It is not universally known, but the organisation was originally founded as the All England Croquet Club and only later in its history did that young upstart lawn tennis inveigle its way into the proceedings. There is still a croquet lawn at the club today, and afficionados will claim that it is an infinitely superior game to the one being played on the courts nearby. It is the quintessential country house game and is generally played on a perfectly groomed stretch of lawn outside the front of the house. A convenient spot, as it means that bitter losers can step straight from the sporting field and in through the French windows of the drawing room to console themselves at the drinks table. And there generally is bitterness to be assuaged, as the game is viciously competitive and largely based on attempts to move one's opponents' balls

Opposite, above: The Duckworth-Chads installed a table tennis table in the entrance hall of Castle Hill during the first COVID lockdown, and it has remained there ever since.

Opposite, below left: A croquet set in Sophie Conran's hallway. In the stick basket is a firework rocket containing her father's ashes.

Opposite, below right: Busts are rarely treated with dignity in the English country house. This sculpture (of the owner's father) is decorated with a feather boa left over from the late queen's last jubilee celebrations. It also provides a perfect stand for a large collection of straw hats.

into unfavourable positions (e.g., a nearby hedge). Every country house that owns a lawn also owns a croquet set, and you will often find its heavy wooden mallets lurking in hall and boot room (rather than put away properly in their smart wooden box). The Duckworth-Chads of Castle Hill in Devon have their own version called "pig croquet," which basically involves playing the game whilst navigating the ball round their two pet pigs, Pinky and Percy.

Another great outdoor sport that makes its mark on the interior of the country house is cricket. If lawns surrounding the house aren't being used for croquet, they might well be the scene of cricket practice, although there is always a slight nervousness that a loosely hit ball might crash through a window of the house. Inside, cricket paraphernalia litters the houses of keen players with cricket bags stored under hall tables, shelves full of *Wisden Cricketers' Almanack* (with its iconic yellow covers), bat oil and mallets for knocking in bats on kitchen tables, brightly striped cricket caps and Panamas with MCC ribbons dotted around, not to mention the downstairs loo of a house we visited in Somerset whose doorknobs have been replaced with old cricket balls.

But more than anything else, the English love horsing around. Country houses are littered with equestrian kit, equine art, and sometimes horses themselves! And if not the living beasts, then the wooden version. We visited dozens of houses in the making of this book, and, almost without exception, all contained a rocking horse; often with a child on board riding it at full gallop in an attempt to make its base skid across the floor.

All in all, fierce game playing and frivolity are as much a part of country house style as Colefax curtains and club fenders.

Left: A bridge table in the drawing room of interior designer Joanna Wood's manor house.

The card table was inherited from her mother, who was "terrifyingly good at bridge."

Above: An embroidered cushion that leaves visiting guests in no doubt as to their obligations. The English love an amusingly sloganed cushion. They often are themed around their owners' schooling (*Good girls go to heaven. Bad girls go to St Mary's Ascot*).

Left: Another bust that doesn't take itself too seriously. This marble lady is wearing a COVID mask and sporting a homemade crown created to celebrate a royal wedding.

Opposite: Marni on her rocking horse in the entrance hall of Bellamont. Her ancestor the first Duke of Devonshire, also on a horse, is mounted above her.

WILLIAM LORD CAVENDISH K.G.
IVTH: A L AND IST: DUKE OF DEVONSHIRE
16 0-1707

Opposite: A teddy bear in the hall of Warmwell—home to Sam Ross-Skinner. The bear is dressed in a page's uniform that Sam's father, as a boy, wore at a family wedding.

Left: This pretty little girl, with her blonde ringlets and blushing pink cheeks, grew up to be Colonel Henry Cartwright—a highly decorated infantry officer—much to the amusement of his descendants. The walking stick that he was using as a hobby horse in this nineteeth-century portrait now hangs below the picture.

Left: Cath Kidston's hall is full of fun pops of colour and also a large portrait of a gentleman in armor. "One year we used a paper hat from a Christmas cracker to cover his bald head, and I've kept it there, as it gives him a jaunty air," says Cath.

Above: A trio of dachshunds (one decorative) below a magnetic darts board in this country house kitchen

Acknowledgements

Writing and photographing this book has been an unqualified pleasure. There are few greater joys than spending time in a beautifully decorated English country house. We are extremely grateful to all the owners who invited us into their homes and allowed us to clank around with our equipment, grill them on the history of their houses, fussily rearrange their cushions, and co-opt their children and dogs into the project. We met some wonderful people (and some fabulous hounds) as we travelled across England. They were all extremely gracious and generous with their time, and spoilt us with all manner of cakes, cocktails, and splendid suppers.

We are also grateful to the many people who suggested houses, effected introductions, and encouraged us in our endeavours.

In particular, we would like to thank Kezzie Acloque, Jeremy Andersen, Emily Archer, Caroline Baker, Leonora Birts, Katy Bolton, Anton Brech, Edward and Emma Bulmer, Emma Burns, John and Shellard Campbell, Freddie and Tanya Cartwright, Jack Cartwright, Frank Chapman, Nina Chin, Mirry Christie, Pandora Cooper-Key, Coco Conran, Sophie Conran, Sophie Crossley, Lindsay Cuthill, Jane Davies, Phoebe Dickinson, Simon and Jessica Dickinson, James and Laura Duckworth-Chad, Tatiana Effingham, Emily Fairweather, Birdie Fortescue, Gina Foster, Christian and Jessica Fleming, Clemmie Fraser, AC Gaskell, Didi Goodenough, Carlos Garcia, Sebastian Gibson, Michael Glendonbrook, Hattie Hansard, James and Lucinda Henderson, Jeff Holland, Amanda Hornby, Charlotte Hepburne-Scott, Caryn Hibbert, Milly Hibbert, Ali Hope, Airlie Inglis, Dominic and Alice Johnson, John Kennedy, Cath Kidston, Elisabeth Krohn, Amy Lim, Henrietta Lindsell, Vanessa Macdonald, Rags Macgregor, James Mackie, Poppy Mahon, Sinead McGill, Diana Muir, Jenny Nicholson, Lauren O'Connor, Georgie Pearman, Patricia Rawlings, Bee Rice, Martin Ritchie, Luke Rodgers, Sam and Serena Ross-Skinner, Evie Sykes, Harriet Sykes, Emma Sims-Hilditch, Nadia Taylor, Katharine Thimbleby, Kasia Turek, Katherine Wickens, Caddy Wilmot-Sitwell, Susan Wells and Joanna Wood.

Finally, we would like to thank our amazing editorial team and publishers at Abrams in New York, in particular Shawna Mullen, Lisa Silverman, and Darilyn Lowe Carnes.

Opposite: Late-season cricket practice on the lawn at Asham House. Jack is about to get out to a ball bowled by his brother.

About the Authors

KATY CAMPBELL is a sought-after property finder based in the Cotswolds. Each year, she travels thousands of miles through the countryside in search of houses for her clients, who range from international celebrities to young families leaving the bustle of the city in search of the Cotswold Dream. From pretty cottages to grand country houses, she specializes in finding off-market properties and has been featured in publications such as the *Times*, *House & Garden*, and *Country Life*. Nearly 100,000 fans follow her adventures on Instagram.
@katy_campbell_house_hunter
www.katycampbell.co.uk

MILO CAMPBELL is a multi-award-winning copywriter and creative director. After a twenty-year career working at some of the world's leading advertising agencies, he moved to the Cotswolds and founded a property search agency with his wife, Katy. He writes about architecture, interiors, and real estate trends and was the co-author of *At Home in the Cotswolds*.
milocampbell@gmail.com

MARK NICHOLSON is an acclaimed photographer based in London and the Cotswolds. He travels worldwide on commissions, and his work has been featured in an international roster of luxury publications, including *House & Garden*, the *Sunday Times*, *Boat International*, and *Country Living*. Nicholson counts the British royal family among his private clients and has photographed many of the great houses of England and Scotland. This is his second collaboration with Milo and Katy Campbell, following the success of their first book, *At Home in the Cotswolds*.
@marknicholson.photographer
www.marknicholson.com

Opposite: The Court of Noke—Edward Bulmer's Queen Anne house in Herefordshire

Editor: Shawna Mullen
Designer: Darilyn Lowe Carnes
Managing Editor: Lisa Silverman
Production Manager: Larry Pekarek

Library of Congress Control Number: 2024933725

ISBN: 978-1-4197-7380-8
eISBN: 979-8-88707-290-6

Printed and bound in China
10 9 8 7 6 5 4 3 2 1

Abrams books are available at special discounts when purchased in quantity for premiums and promotions as well as fundraising or educational use. Special editions can also be created to specification. For details, contact specialsales@abramsbooks.com or the address below.

Abrams® is a registered trademark of Harry N. Abrams, Inc.

ABRAMS
The Art of Books

195 Broadway
New York, NY 10007
abramsbooks.com